BEETLE BAILEY: LET'S GRAB A BITE!

Here's another in the happy series of books based on one of the most famous comic strips in the country. Once again the madcap inmates of Camp Swampy valiantly strive to overcome their own ineptitude — and succeed in delighting us on every page.

Mort Walker again gives us a barrel of laughs in his marvelous cartoons concerning the most unprofessional soldier in the army!

Beetle Bailey Books

ABOUT FACE, BEETLE BAILEY
AT EASE, BEETLE BAILEY
BEETLE BAILEY: ANOTHER REQUEST FOR FURLOUGH
BEETLE BAILEY: BASKET CASE
BEETLE BAILEY HARD KNOCKS
BEETLE BAILEY: LET'S GRAB A BITE!
BEETLE BAILEY: NEW OUTFIT!
BEETLE BAILEY ON PARADE
BEETLE BAILEY: OPERATION GOOD TIMES
BEETLE BAILEY: TABLE SERVICE
BEETLE BAILEY: WIPED OUT
BEETLE BAILEY: WORLD'S LAZIEST PRIVATE
BIG HITS FROM BEETLE BAILEY
DID YOU FIX THE BRAKES, BEETLE BAILEY
DON'T MAKE ME LAUGH, BEETLE BAILEY
FALL OUT LAUGHING, BEETLE BAILEY
GIVE US A SMILE, BEETLE BAILEY
I DON'T WANT TO BE OUT HERE
ANY MORE THAN YOU DO, BEETLE BAILEY
I'LL FLIP YOU FOR IT, BEETLE BAILEY
I JUST WANT TO TALK TO YOU, BEETLE BAILEY
IS THAT ALL, BEETLE BAILEY
IS THIS ANOTHER COMPLAINT, BEETLE BAILEY?
I'VE GOT YOU ON MY LIST, BEETLE BAILEY
LET'S CHANGE PLACES, BEETLE BAILEY
LOOKIN' GOOD, BEETLE BAILEY
OTTO
PEACE, BEETLE BAILEY
SHAPE UP OR SHIP OUT, BEETLE BAILEY
TAKE A WALK, BEETLE BAILEY
TAKE TEN, BEETLE BAILEY
WE'RE ALL IN THE SAME BOAT, BEETLE BAILEY
WHAT IS IT NOW, BEETLE BAILEY?
WHAT'S THE JOKE, BEETLE BAILEY?
WHO'S IN CHARGE HERE, BEETLE BAILEY?
WOULD IT HELP TO SAY I'M SORRY, BEETLE BAILEY?
YOU'LL GET A BANG OUT OF THIS, BEETLE BAILEY
YOU'RE OUT OF HUP, BEETLE BAILEY?
YOU'RE ALL WASHED UP, BEETLE BAILEY

beetle bailey
LET'S GRAB A BITE!

Mort Walker

JOVE BOOKS, NEW YORK

BEETLE BAILEY: LET'S GRAB A BITE!

A Jove Book / published by arrangement with
King Features Syndicate, Inc.

PRINTING HISTORY
Jove edition / May 1991

All rights reserved.
Copyright © 1988, 1991 by King Features Syndicate, Inc.
This book may not be reproduced in whole or in part,
by mimeograph or any other means, without permission.
For information address: The Berkley Publishing Group,
200 Madison Avenue, New York, New York 10016.

ISBN: 0-515-10575-9

Jove Books are published by The Berkley Publishing Group,
200 Madison Avenue, New York, New York 10016.
The name "JOVE" and the "J" logo
are trademarks belonging to Jove Publications, Inc.

PRINTED IN THE UNITED STATES OF AMERICA

10 9 8 7 6 5 4 3 2 1

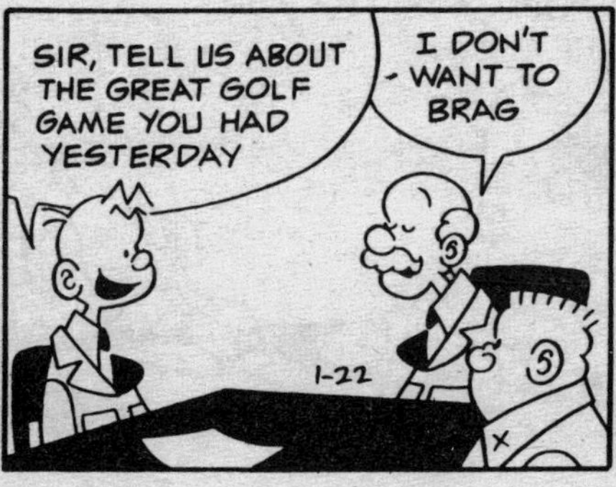
SIR, TELL US ABOUT THE GREAT GOLF GAME YOU HAD YESTERDAY
I DON'T WANT TO BRAG
1-22

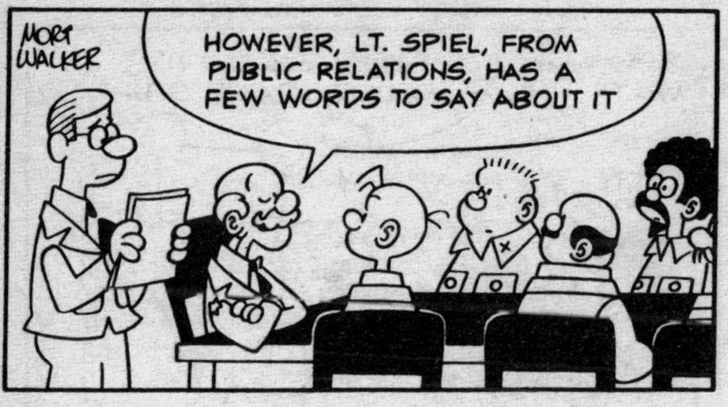
MORT WALKER
HOWEVER, LT. SPIEL, FROM PUBLIC RELATIONS, HAS A FEW WORDS TO SAY ABOUT IT

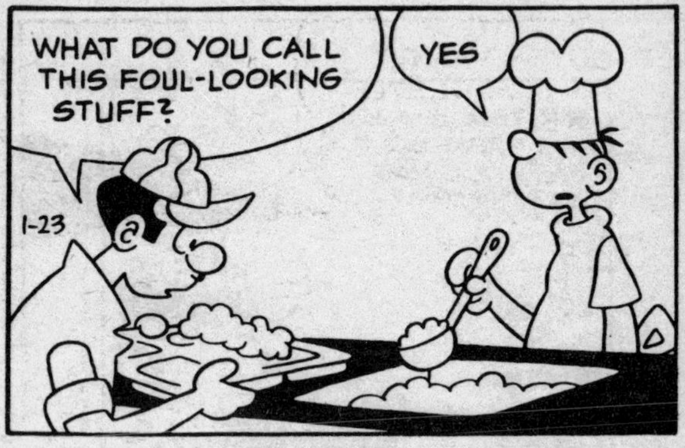
WHAT DO YOU CALL THIS FOUL-LOOKING STUFF?
YES
1-23

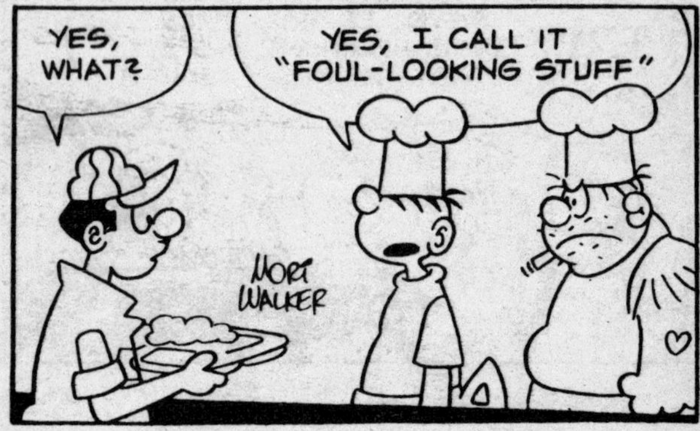
YES, WHAT?
YES, I CALL IT "FOUL-LOOKING STUFF"
MORT WALKER

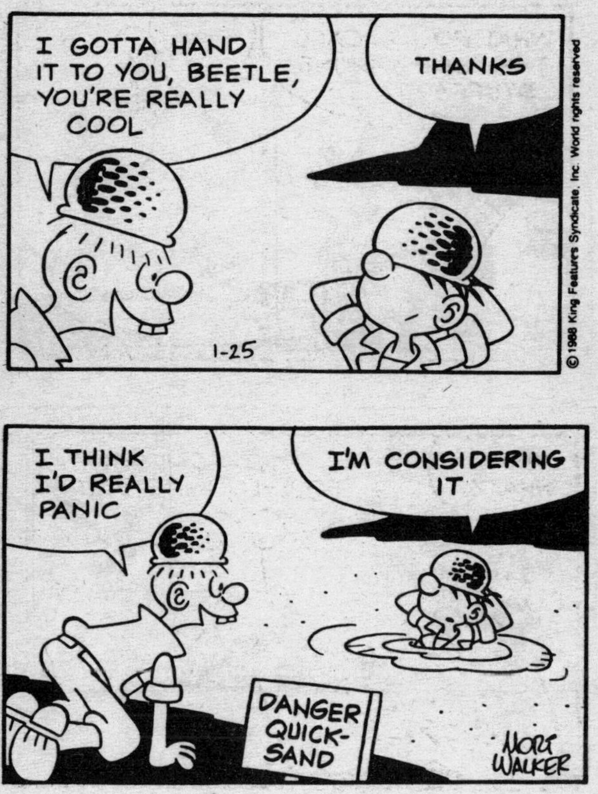
I GOTTA HAND IT TO YOU, BEETLE, YOU'RE REALLY COOL
THANKS
1-25
© 1988 King Features Syndicate, Inc. World rights reserved
I THINK I'D REALLY PANIC
I'M CONSIDERING IT
DANGER QUICK-SAND
MORT WALKER

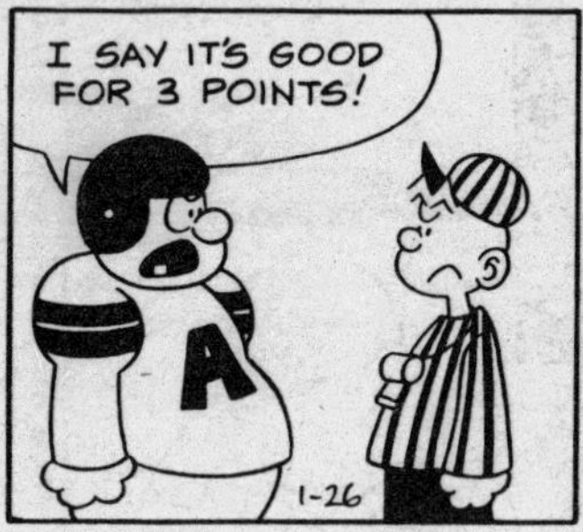
I SAY IT'S GOOD FOR 3 POINTS!
1-26

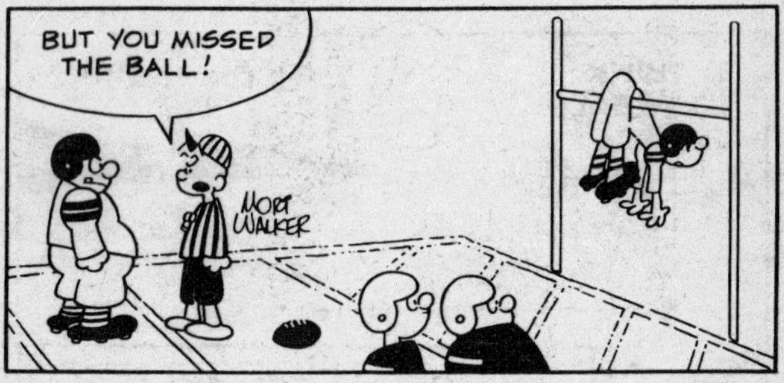
BUT YOU MISSED THE BALL!
MORT WALKER

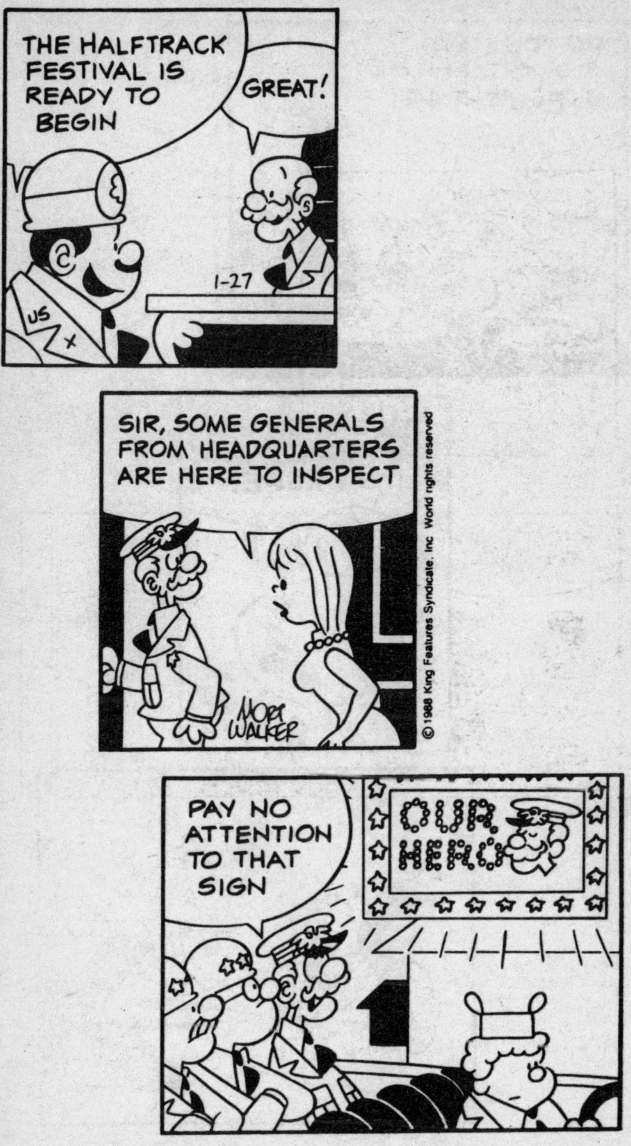
THE HALFTRACK FESTIVAL IS READY TO BEGIN
GREAT!
1-27
SIR, SOME GENERALS FROM HEADQUARTERS ARE HERE TO INSPECT
MORT WALKER
PAY NO ATTENTION TO THAT SIGN
OUR HERO

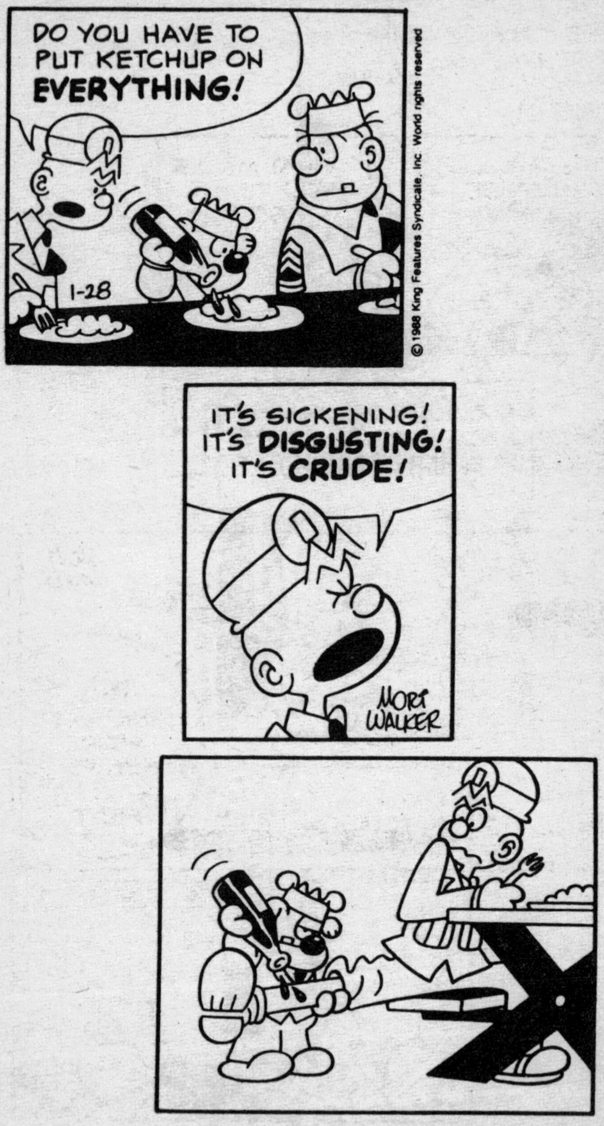
DO YOU HAVE TO PUT KETCHUP ON **EVERYTHING**!
1-28
© 1988 King Features Syndicate, Inc. World rights reserved
IT'S SICKENING! IT'S **DISGUSTING**! IT'S **CRUDE**!
MORT WALKER

THESE GAUGES MUST BE BROKEN
WHAT MAKES YOU THINK SO?
NORI WALKER
THIS ONE SAYS WE'RE FLYING AT 200 FEET
1-29

BEETLE IS THE IDEAL FROGMAN
1-30
© 1988 King Features Syndicate, Inc. World rights reserved
MORT WALKER
HE'D RATHER SINK THAN SWIM

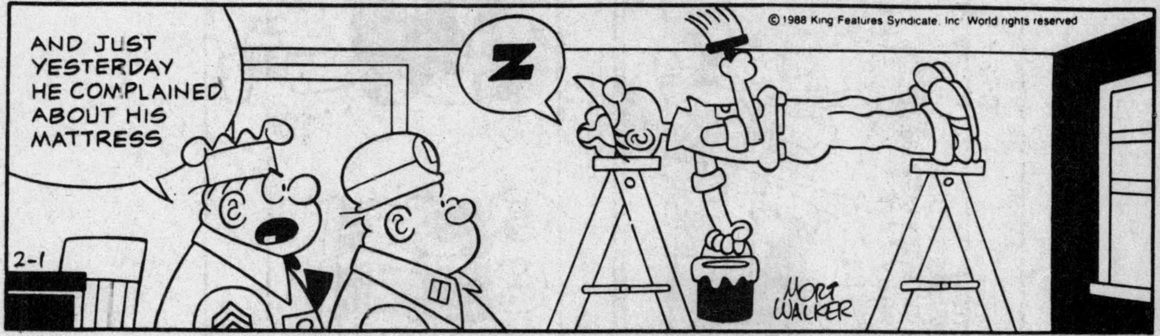
AND JUST YESTERDAY HE COMPLAINED ABOUT HIS MATTRESS
Z
2-1
MORT WALKER
© 1988 King Features Syndicate, Inc. World rights reserved

LOUISE LUGG SURE TOOK THAT GUY OUT
WHAT MADE HER SO MAD?
2-2
©1988 King Features Syndicate, Inc. World rights reserved
HE BROKE HER FINGER-NAIL
MORT WALKER

WOULD YOU LIKE TO GO TO A POOL PARTY AND MEET A FAMOUS CELEBRITY?
LOVE TO!
2-3
MINNESOTA FATS, MEET MISS BUXLEY
MORT WALKER

STOP THAT, LT. FUZZ! I TOLD YOU BEFORE, THAT'S NOT NECESSARY!
2-4
© 1988 King Features Syndicate, Inc. World rights reserved
MORT WALKER
NOW, HOLD ON, CAPTAIN...

THIS TEST WILL BE GIVEN ON THE HONOR SYSTEM
I'LL LEAVE YOU NOW WITH YOUR CONSCIENCE
2-5
WHAT A DIRTY TRICK
I STAYED UP ALL NIGHT TO STUDY AND HE'LL NEVER BELIEVE I DIDN'T CHEAT
MORT WALKER

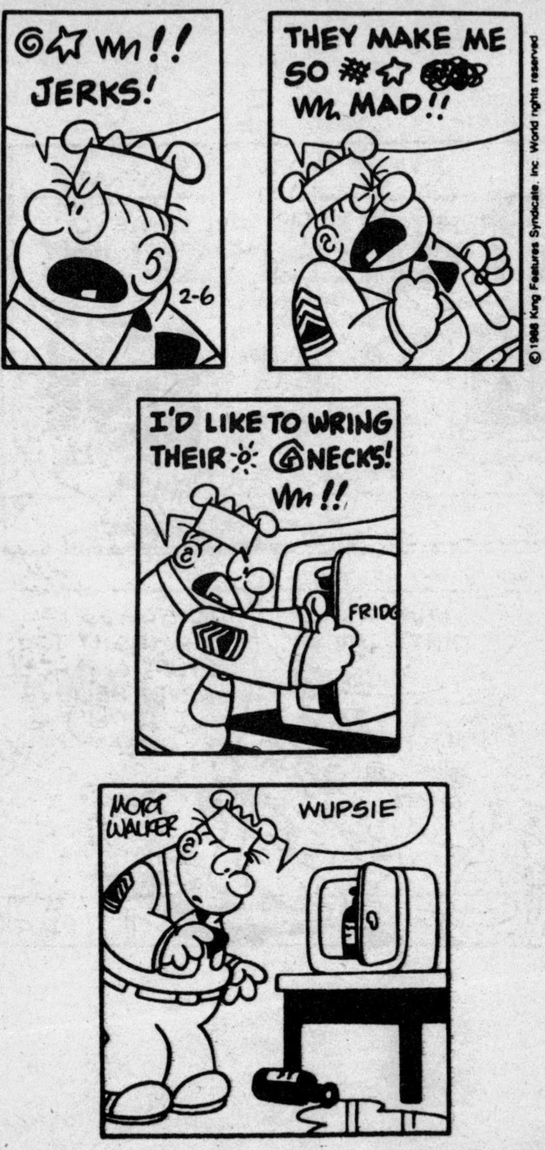
JERKS!
2-6
THEY MAKE ME SO MAD!!
© 1988 King Features Syndicate, Inc. World rights reserved
I'D LIKE TO WRING THEIR NECKS!
FRIDG
MORT WALKER
WUPSIE

I WANT 110% GROUP EFFORT ON THIS MEN
WHAT DOES HE MEAN "110%"?
2-8
WE GIVE 100% AND BEETLE GIVES 10%
MORT WALKER

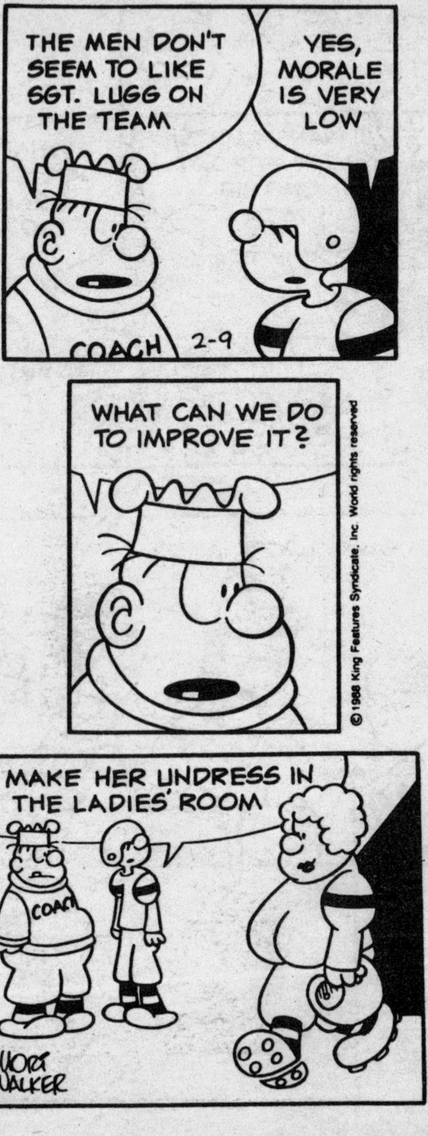
THE MEN DON'T SEEM TO LIKE SGT. LUGG ON THE TEAM
YES, MORALE IS VERY LOW
COACH
2-9
WHAT CAN WE DO TO IMPROVE IT?
MAKE HER UNDRESS IN THE LADIES' ROOM
COACH
MORT WALKER

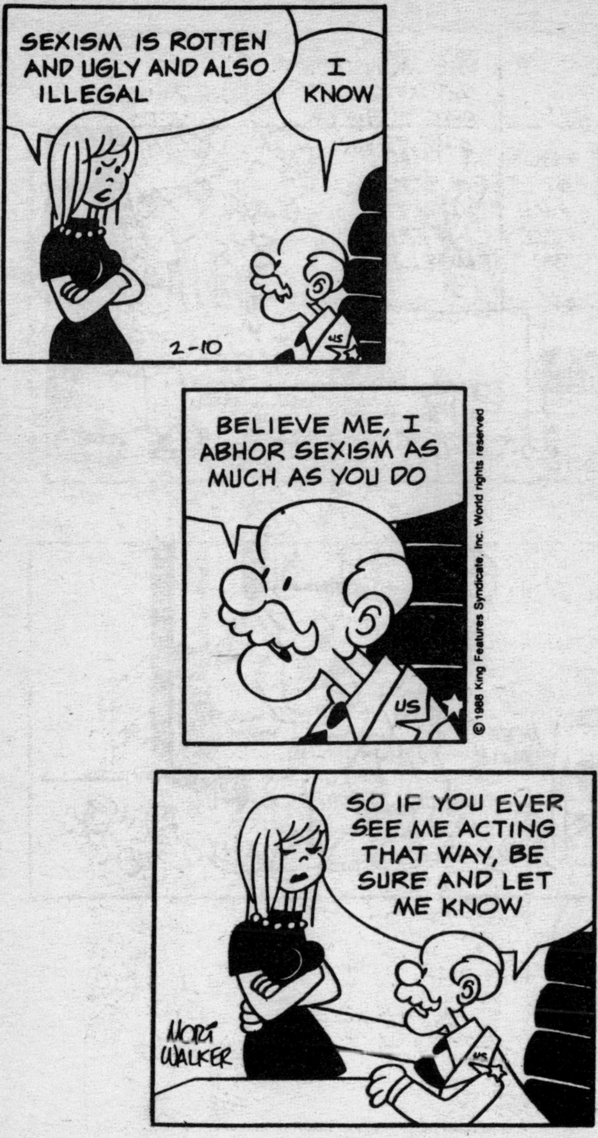
SEXISM IS ROTTEN AND UGLY AND ALSO ILLEGAL
I KNOW
2-10
BELIEVE ME, I ABHOR SEXISM AS MUCH AS YOU DO
SO IF YOU EVER SEE ME ACTING THAT WAY, BE SURE AND LET ME KNOW
MORT WALKER

LOOK AT THAT! BEETLE'S SOCKS ARE SO DIRTY THEY CAN STAND BY THEMSELVES!
2-11
©1988 King Features Syndicate, Inc. World rights reserved
MORT WALKER

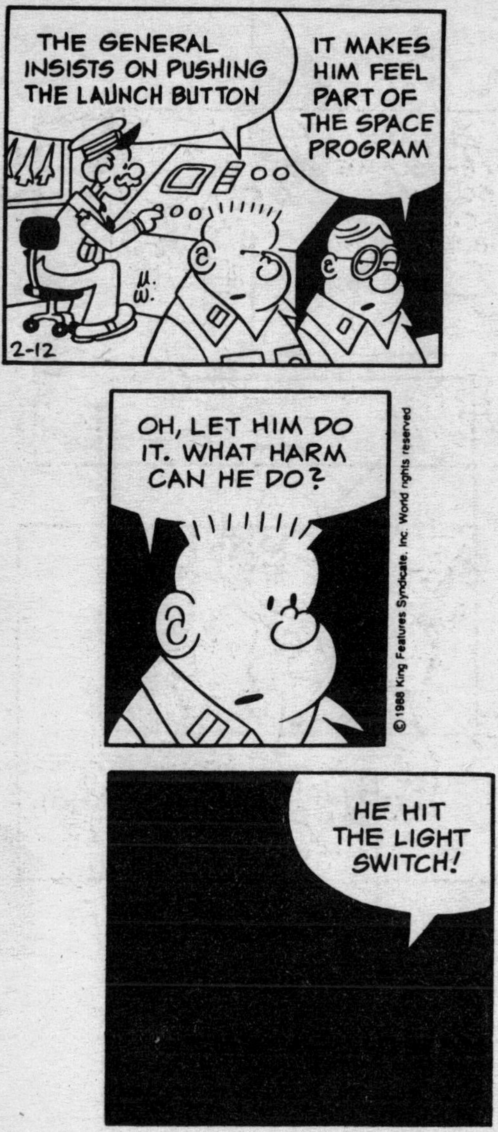
THE GENERAL INSISTS ON PUSHING THE LAUNCH BUTTON
IT MAKES HIM FEEL PART OF THE SPACE PROGRAM
2-12
OH, LET HIM DO IT. WHAT HARM CAN HE DO?
© 1988 King Features Syndicate, Inc. World rights reserved
HE HIT THE LIGHT SWITCH!

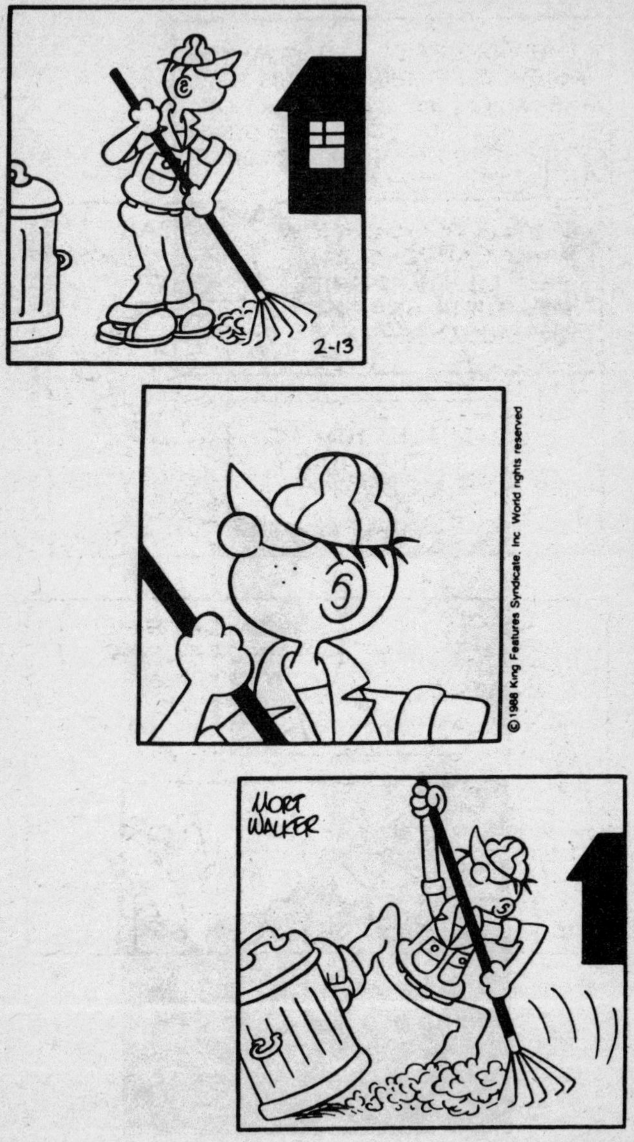
2-13
MORT
WALKER

BEETLE, DO YOU KNOW WHAT HAPPENS TO PEOPLE WHO DON'T USE THEIR BRAINS OR MUSCLES?
YEAH
2-15
©1988 King Features Syndicate, Inc. World rights reserved
THEY GET SENT TO OFFICERS' TRAINING SCHOOL
MORT WALKER

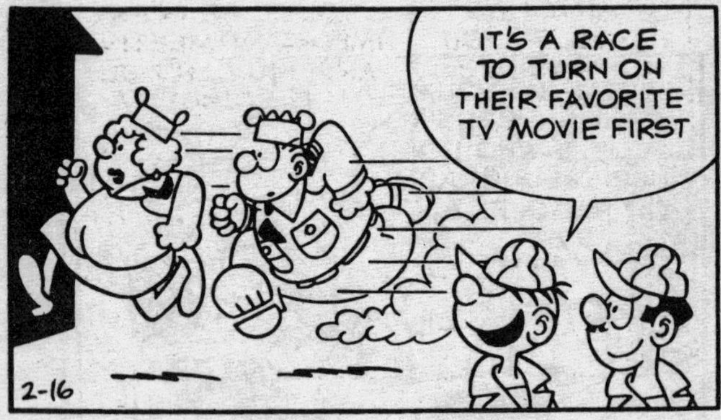
IT'S A RACE TO TURN ON THEIR FAVORITE TV MOVIE FIRST
2-16

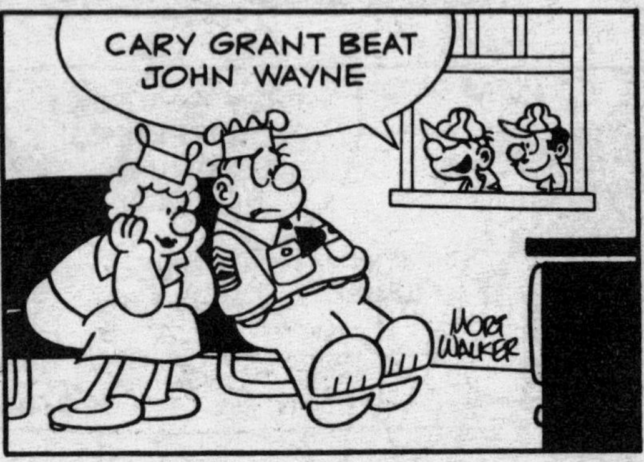
CARY GRANT BEAT JOHN WAYNE
MORT WALKER

IF ANYONE CALLS, DO YOU KNOW WHERE I'LL BE?
YOU'LL BE IN AN IMPORTANT MEETING AND YOU CAN'T BE DISTURBED
US
2-17
NO ONE WILL EVER CALL HER A DUMB BLONDE
MORT WALKER

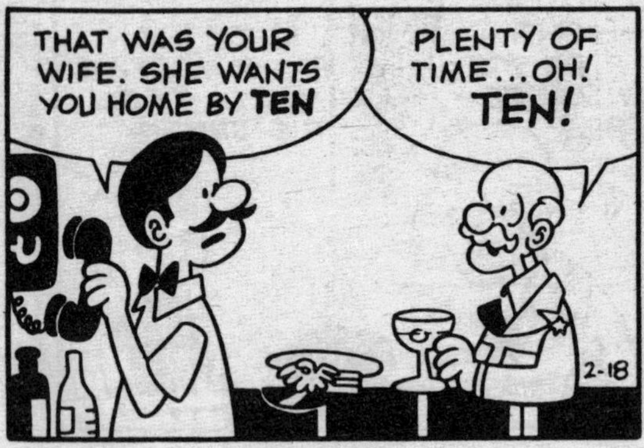
THAT WAS YOUR WIFE. SHE WANTS YOU HOME BY TEN
PLENTY OF TIME...OH! TEN!
2-18

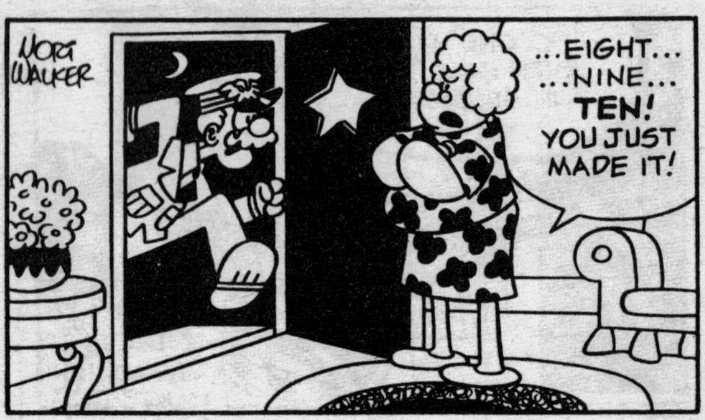
NORT WALKER
...EIGHT... ...NINE... TEN! YOU JUST MADE IT!

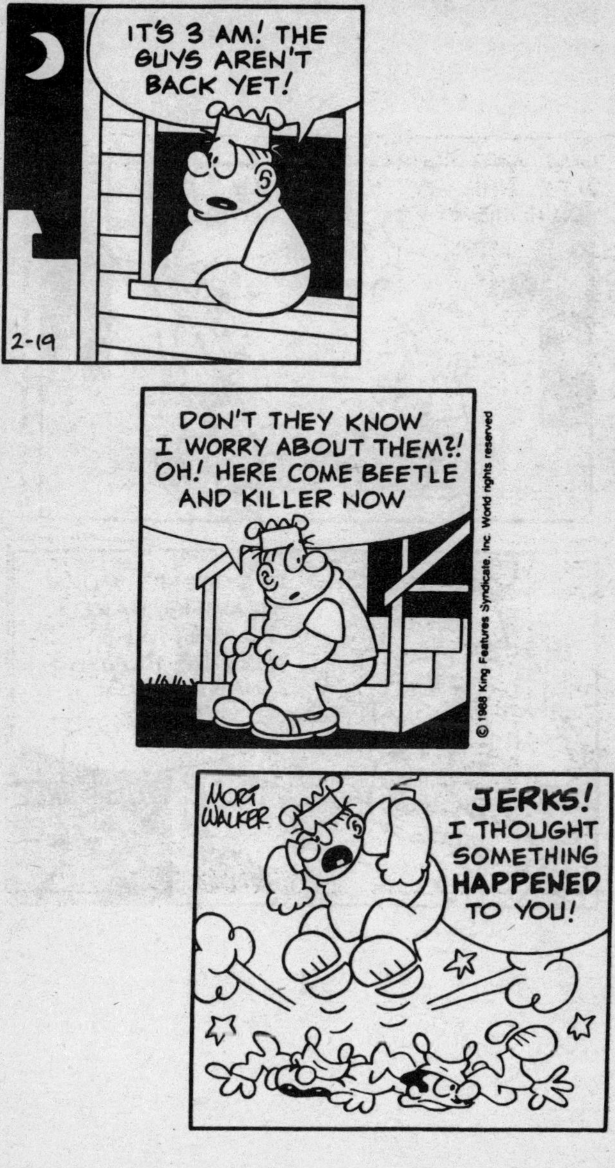
IT'S 3 AM! THE GUYS AREN'T BACK YET!
2-19
DON'T THEY KNOW I WORRY ABOUT THEM?! OH! HERE COME BEETLE AND KILLER NOW
MORT WALKER
JERKS! I THOUGHT SOMETHING HAPPENED TO YOU!

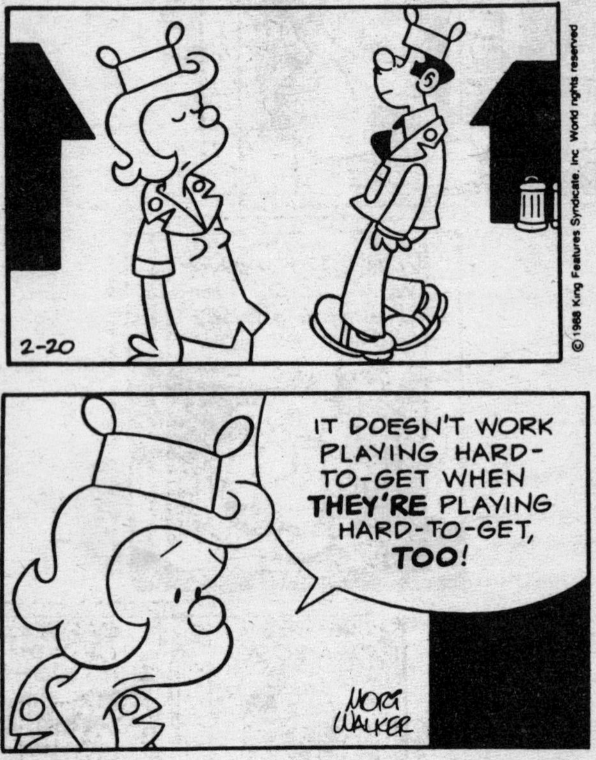
2-20
IT DOESN'T WORK PLAYING HARD-TO-GET WHEN **THEY'RE** PLAYING HARD-TO-GET, **TOO**!
MORT WALKER

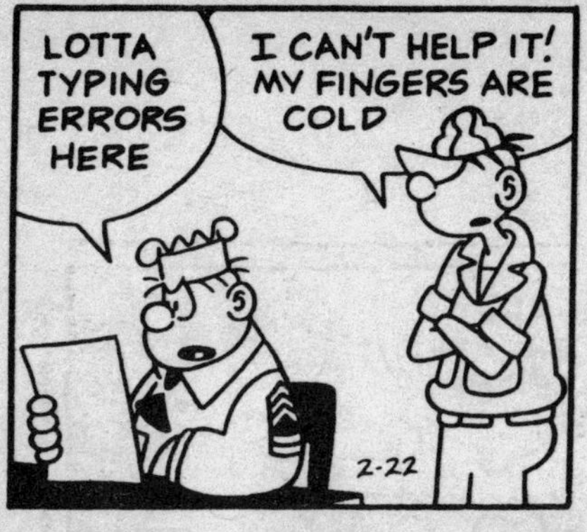
LOTTA TYPING ERRORS HERE
I CAN'T HELP IT! MY FINGERS ARE COLD
2-22

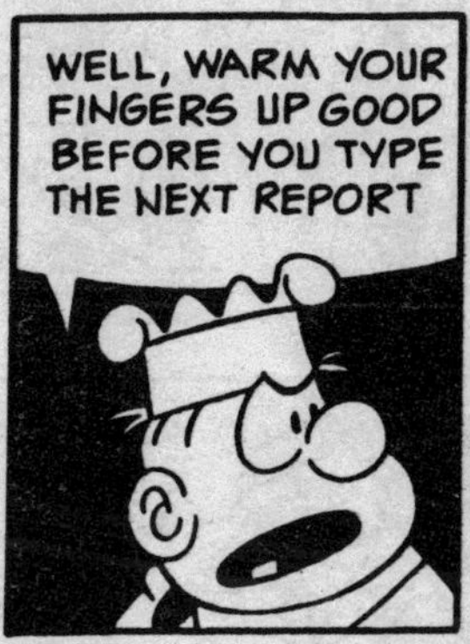
WELL, WARM YOUR FINGERS UP GOOD BEFORE YOU TYPE THE NEXT REPORT

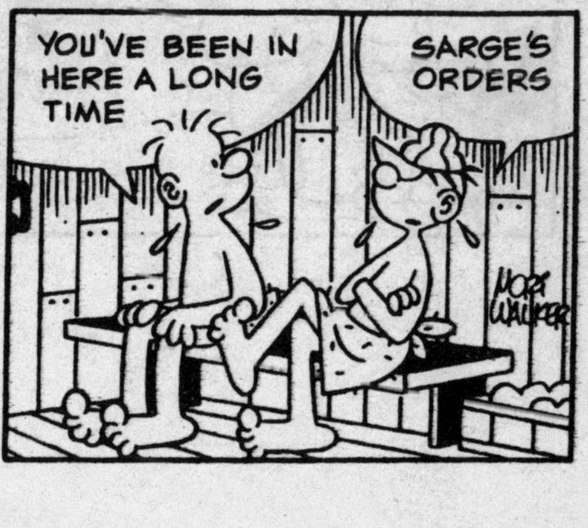
YOU'VE BEEN IN HERE A LONG TIME
SARGE'S ORDERS
MORT WALKER

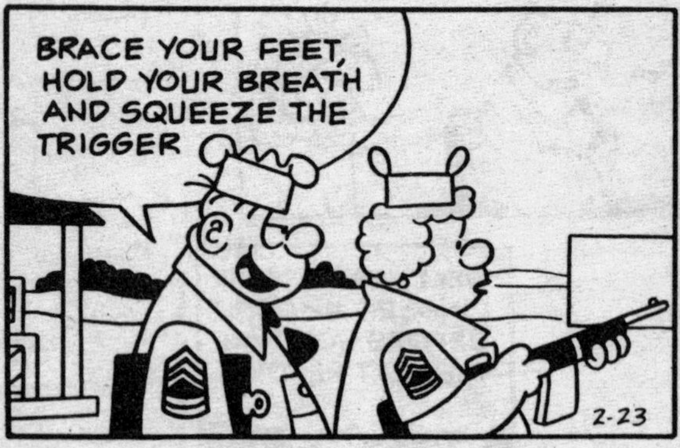
BRACE YOUR FEET, HOLD YOUR BREATH AND SQUEEZE THE TRIGGER
2-23

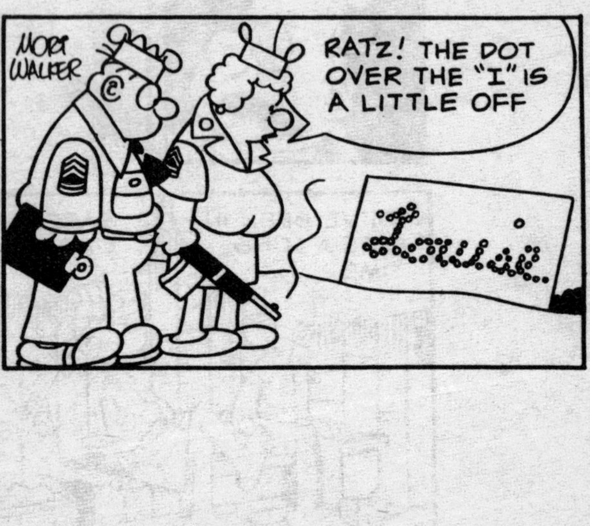
MORT WALKER
RATZ! THE DOT OVER THE "I" IS A LITTLE OFF
Louise

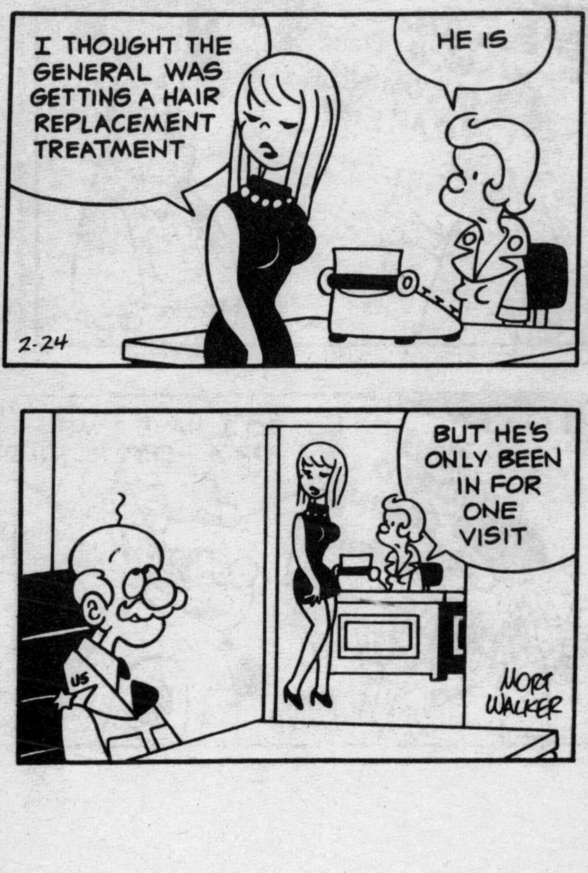
I THOUGHT THE GENERAL WAS GETTING A HAIR REPLACEMENT TREATMENT
HE IS
2-24
BUT HE'S ONLY BEEN IN FOR ONE VISIT
US
MORT WALKER

THE WORLD IS COMING TO AN END
2-25
THE WORLD S COMING AN END
DO I HAVE TIME FOR A PEPPERONI PIZZA?
MORT WALKER

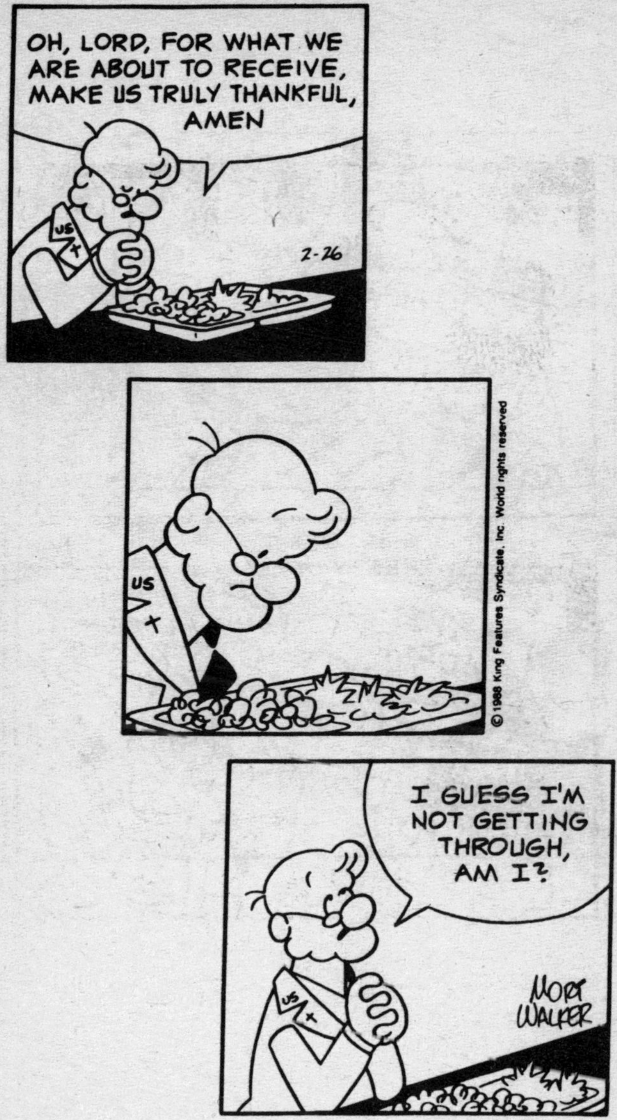
OH, LORD, FOR WHAT WE ARE ABOUT TO RECEIVE, MAKE US TRULY THANKFUL, AMEN
2-26
I GUESS I'M NOT GETTING THROUGH, AM I?
MORT WALKER

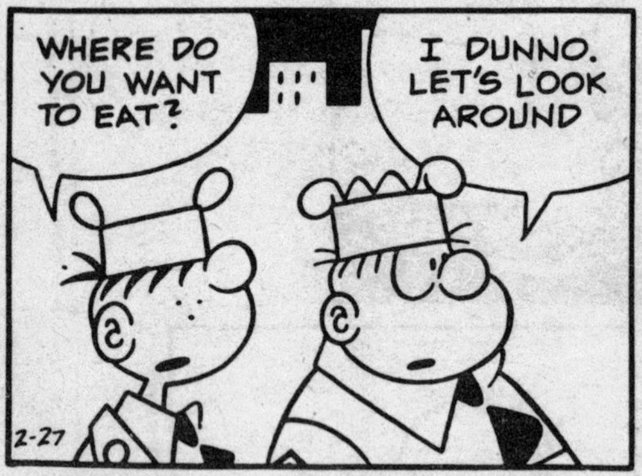
WHERE DO YOU WANT TO EAT?
I DUNNO. LET'S LOOK AROUND
2-27

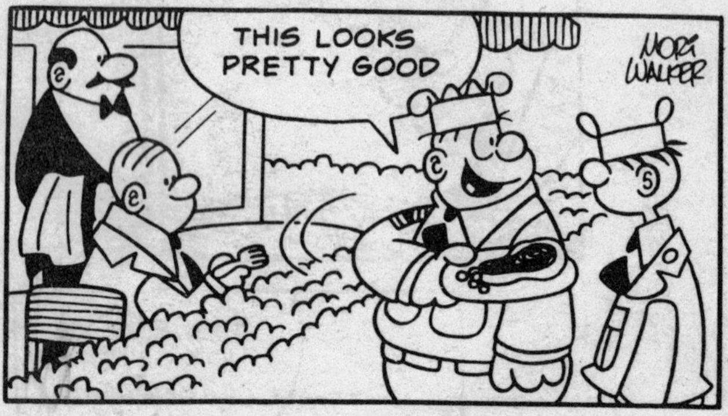
THIS LOOKS PRETTY GOOD
MORT WALKER

BEETLE! WHAT ARE YOU DOING ?!
I'M GOOFING OFF, YOU BIG DUMBBELL, WHAT DO YOU THINK I'M DOING?!
2-29
MORT WALKER
IT'S MEAN TO CONFUSE HIM LIKE THAT, BEETLE

MY SECRET FANTASY IS TO HAVE TWO MEN FIGHT OVER ME
WE CAN ARRANGE THAT
3-1
© 1988 King Features Syndicate, Inc. World rights reserved
OKAY, LIE DOWN RIGHT THERE
MORT WALKER

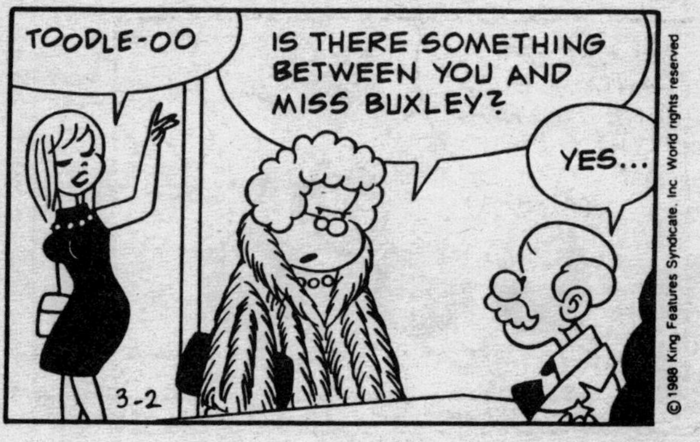
TOODLE-OO
IS THERE SOMETHING BETWEEN YOU AND MISS BUXLEY?
YES...
3-2
© 1988 King Features Syndicate, Inc. World rights reserved

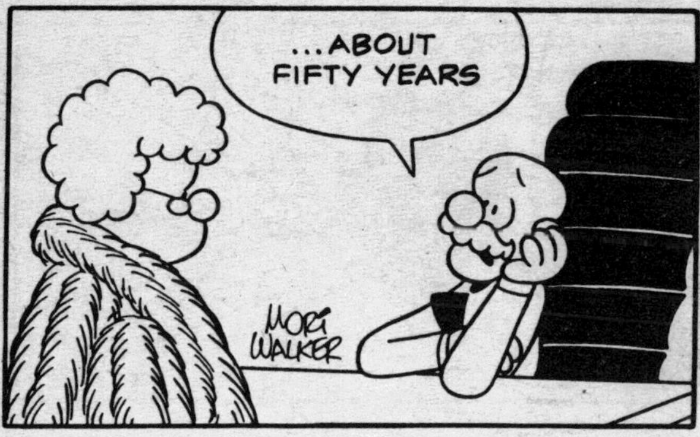
...ABOUT FIFTY YEARS
MORT WALKER

WHY ARE YOU SPEEDING, ZERO?
WE'RE ALMOST OUT OF GAS
3-3
I'M TRYING TO GET BACK TO CAMP BEFORE THE TANK IS EMPTY
MORT WALKER

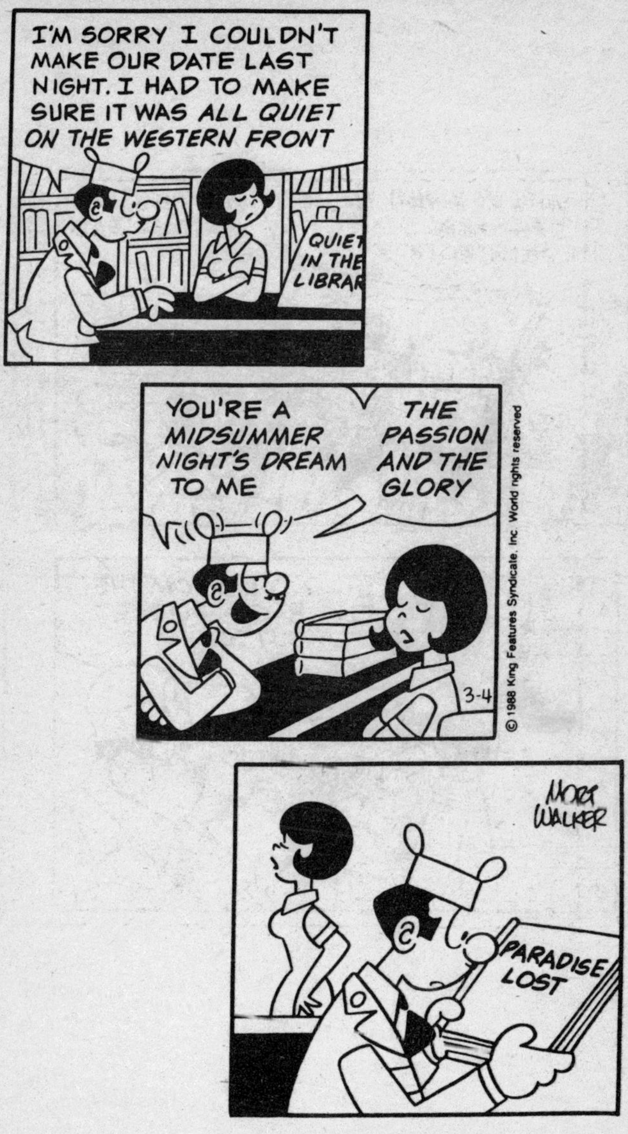
I'M SORRY I COULDN'T MAKE OUR DATE LAST NIGHT. I HAD TO MAKE SURE IT WAS ALL QUIET ON THE WESTERN FRONT
QUIET IN THE LIBRAR
YOU'RE A MIDSUMMER NIGHT'S DREAM TO ME
THE PASSION AND THE GLORY
3-4
MORT WALKER
PARADISE LOST

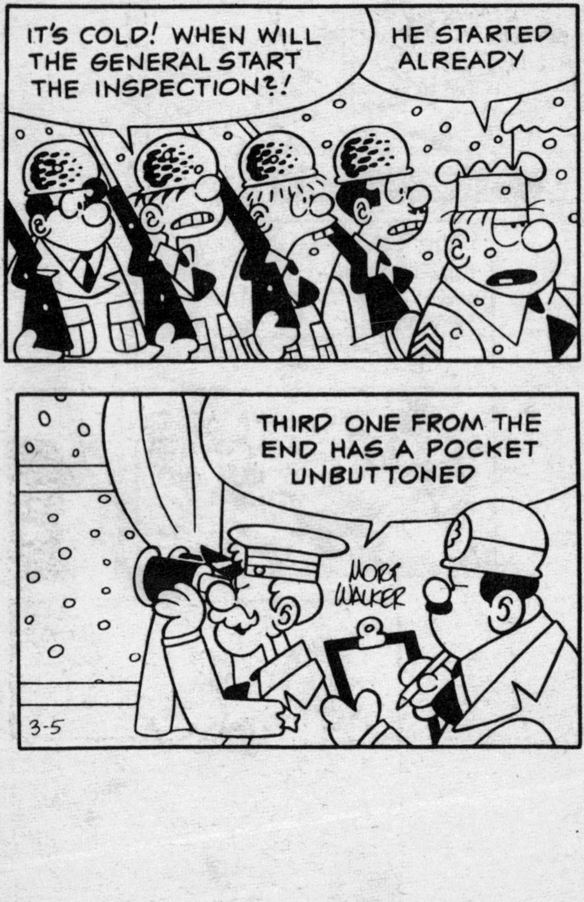
IT'S COLD! WHEN WILL THE GENERAL START THE INSPECTION?!
HE STARTED ALREADY
THIRD ONE FROM THE END HAS A POCKET UNBUTTONED
MORT WALKER
3-5

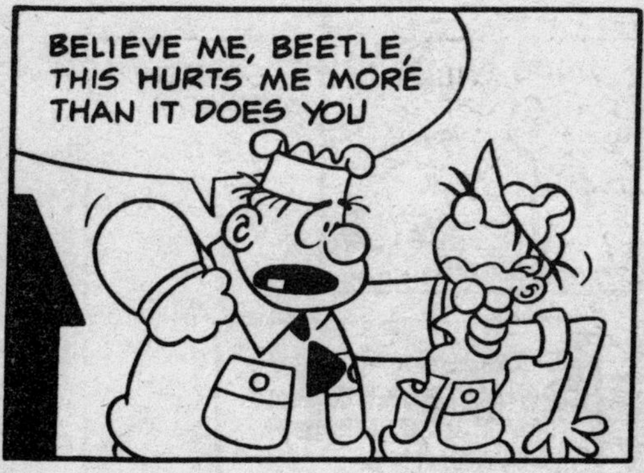
BELIEVE ME, BEETLE, THIS HURTS ME MORE THAN IT DOES YOU

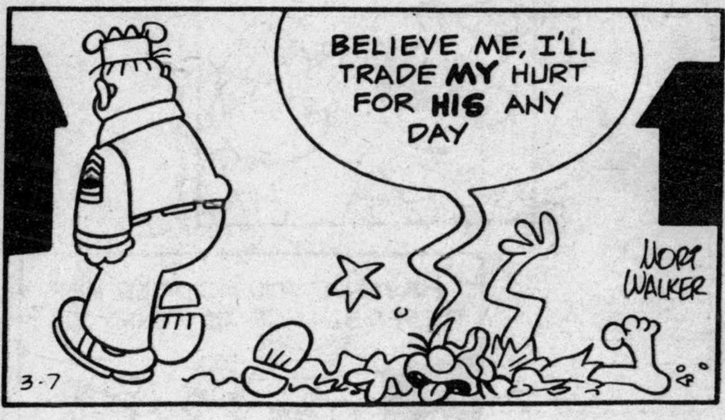
BELIEVE ME, I'LL TRADE **MY** HURT FOR **HIS** ANY DAY
MORT WALKER
3-7

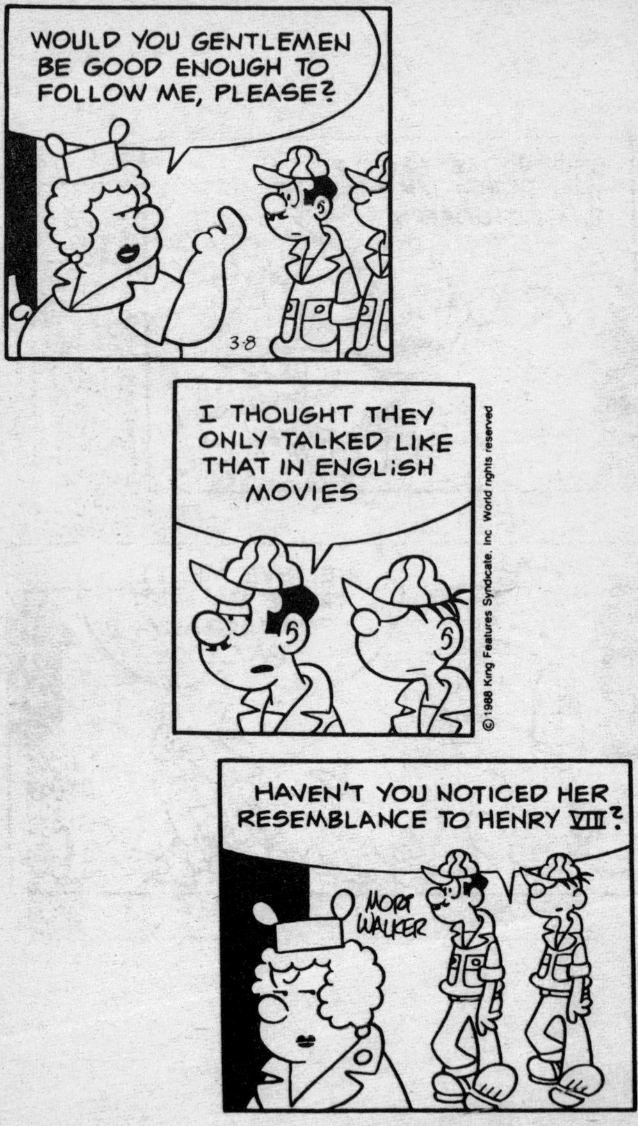
WOULD YOU GENTLEMEN BE GOOD ENOUGH TO FOLLOW ME, PLEASE?
3-8
I THOUGHT THEY ONLY TALKED LIKE THAT IN ENGLiSH MOVIES
HAVEN'T YOU NOTICED HER RESEMBLANCE TO HENRY VIII?
MORT WALKER

LIEUTENANT, I EXPECT YOU TO MAKE PLANS AND STICK TO THEM
DON'T GET SIDE-TRACKED OR CONFUSED...
3-9
SIR...
ER...UH... I'LL CALL YOU BACK!
MORT WALKER

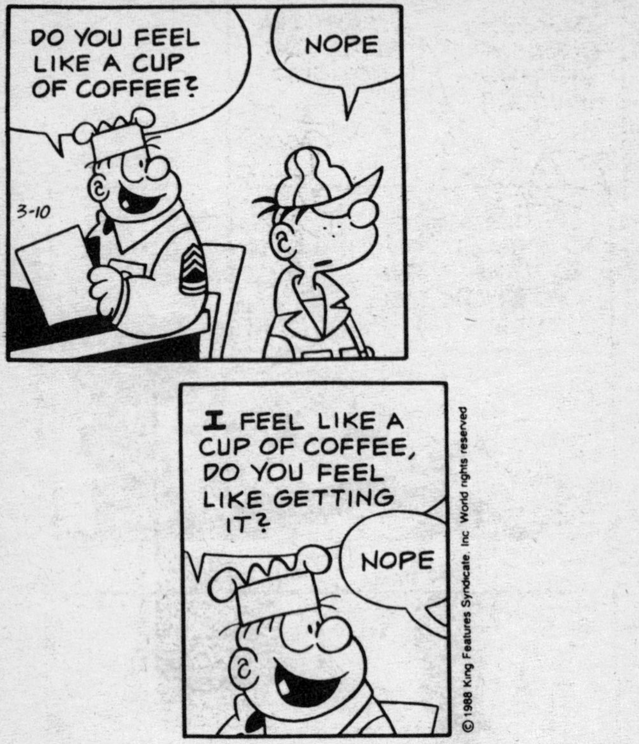
DO YOU FEEL LIKE A CUP OF COFFEE?
NOPE
3-10
I FEEL LIKE A CUP OF COFFEE, DO YOU FEEL LIKE GETTING IT?
NOPE
DO YOU FEEL LIKE GETTING CLOBBERED?
Y'KNOW, I LIKE IT MORE WHEN YOU JUST GIVE ORDERS
MORT WALKER

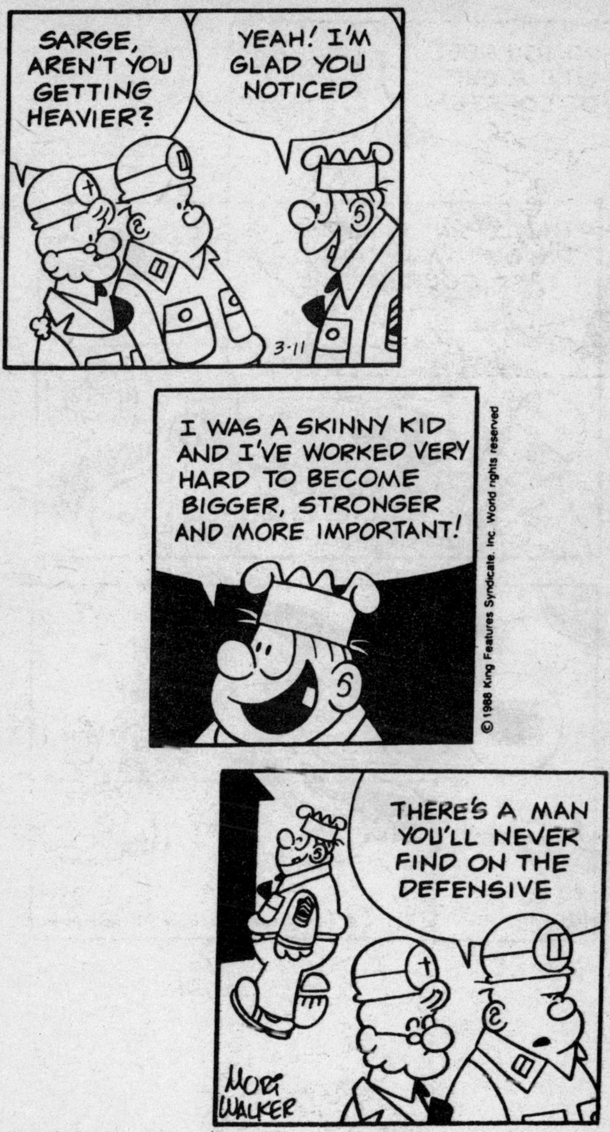
SARGE, AREN'T YOU GETTING HEAVIER?
YEAH! I'M GLAD YOU NOTICED
3-11
I WAS A SKINNY KID AND I'VE WORKED VERY HARD TO BECOME BIGGER, STRONGER AND MORE IMPORTANT!
THERE'S A MAN YOU'LL NEVER FIND ON THE DEFENSIVE
MORT WALKER

THEY SPENT BILLIONS ON THAT WEAPON BUT THEY GOOFED
3-12
HOW?
MORT WALKER
© 1988 King Features Syndicate, Inc. World rights reserved

WHAT KIND OF CAMOUFLAGE IS THAT, BEETLE?!
URBAN WARFARE
3-14
©1988 King Features Syndicate, Inc. World rights reserved
MORT WALKER

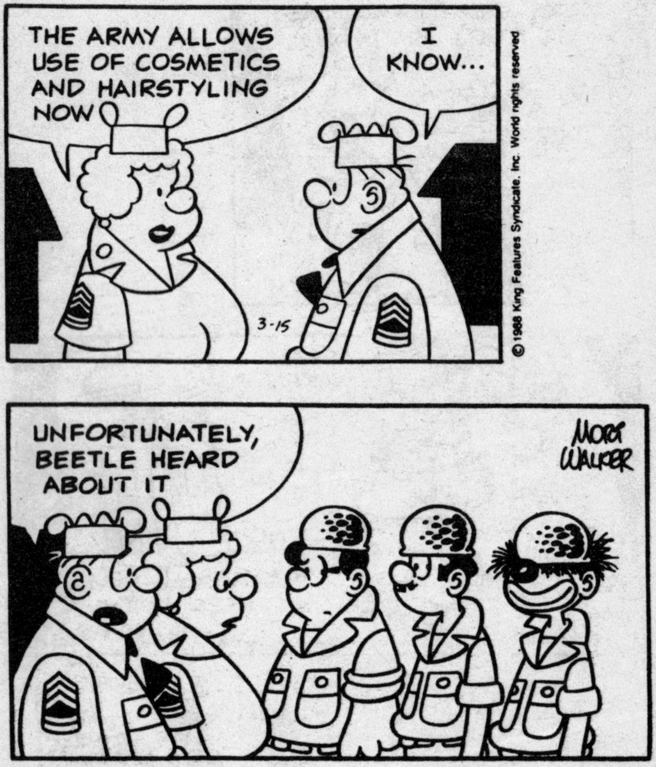
THE ARMY ALLOWS USE OF COSMETICS AND HAIRSTYLING NOW
I KNOW...
3-15
UNFORTUNATELY, BEETLE HEARD ABOUT IT
MORT WALKER

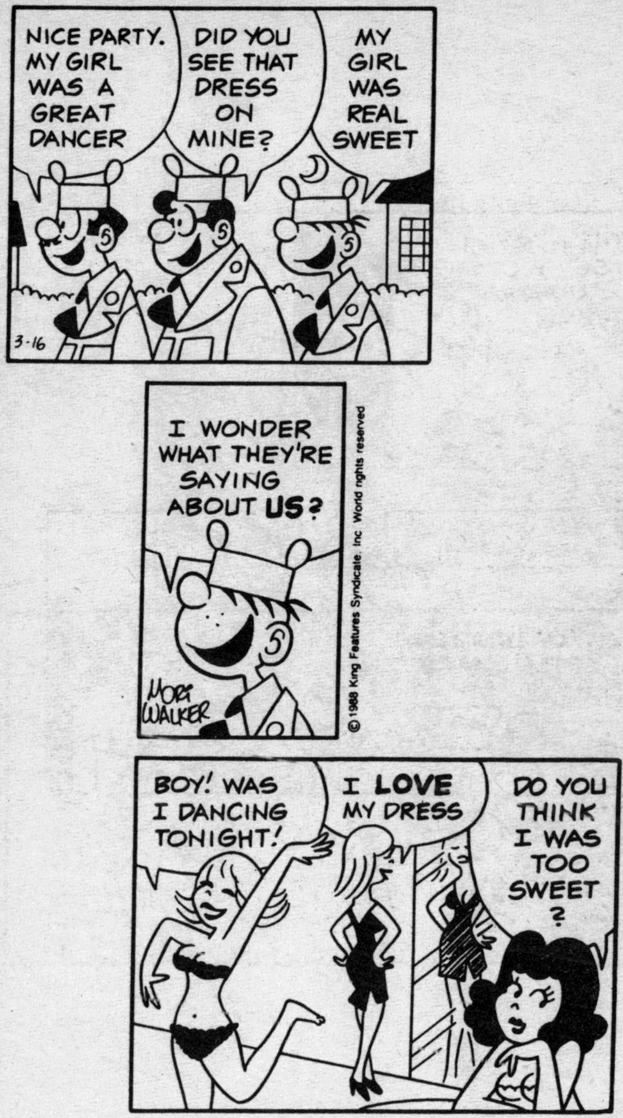
3-16
NICE PARTY. MY GIRL WAS A GREAT DANCER
DID YOU SEE THAT DRESS ON MINE?
MY GIRL WAS REAL SWEET
I WONDER WHAT THEY'RE SAYING ABOUT **US**?
MORT WALKER
BOY! WAS I DANCING TONIGHT!
I **LOVE** MY DRESS
DO YOU THINK I WAS TOO SWEET?

THE DINING HALL HAS A NO-SMOKING SECTION NOW
"A" CO. DINING HALL
3 17
WHAT DIFFERENCE DOES IT MAKE?
MORT WALKER

I HAVE TO GO TO THE BATH-ROOM
THERE'S A JOHN IN THE ENLISTED MEN'S CLUB
EM CLUB
3-18
HEY! LOOK WHO THINKS THEY'RE SOMEBODY
GENTLEMEN
MORT WALKER

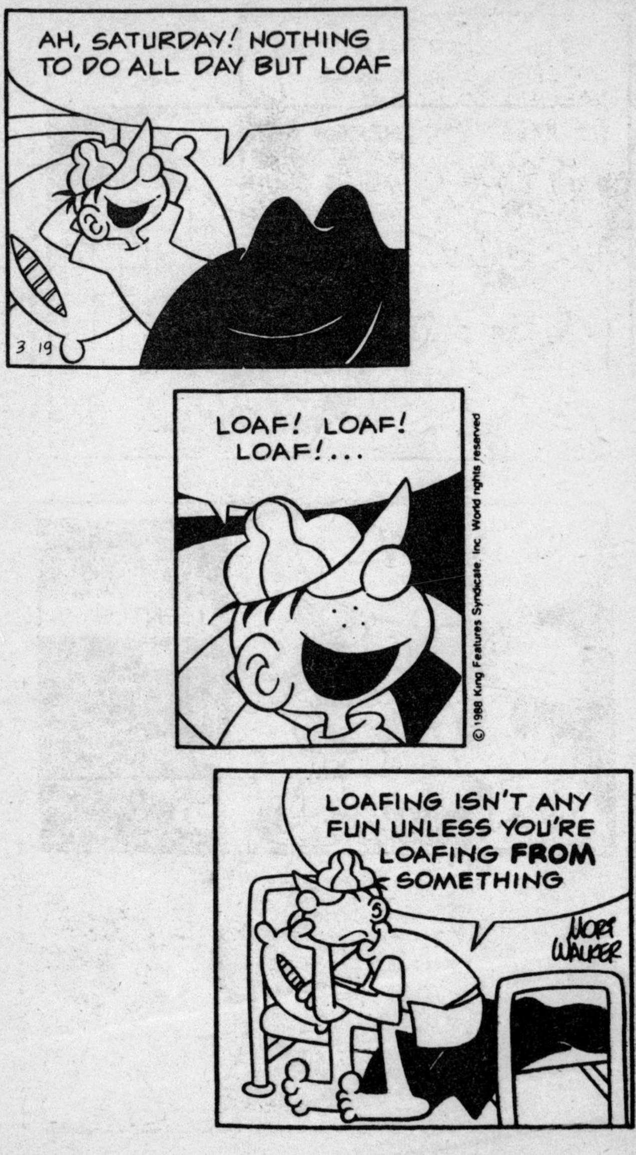
AH, SATURDAY! NOTHING TO DO ALL DAY BUT LOAF
3 19
LOAF! LOAF! LOAF!...
LOAFING ISN'T ANY FUN UNLESS YOU'RE LOAFING **FROM** SOMETHING
MORT WALKER

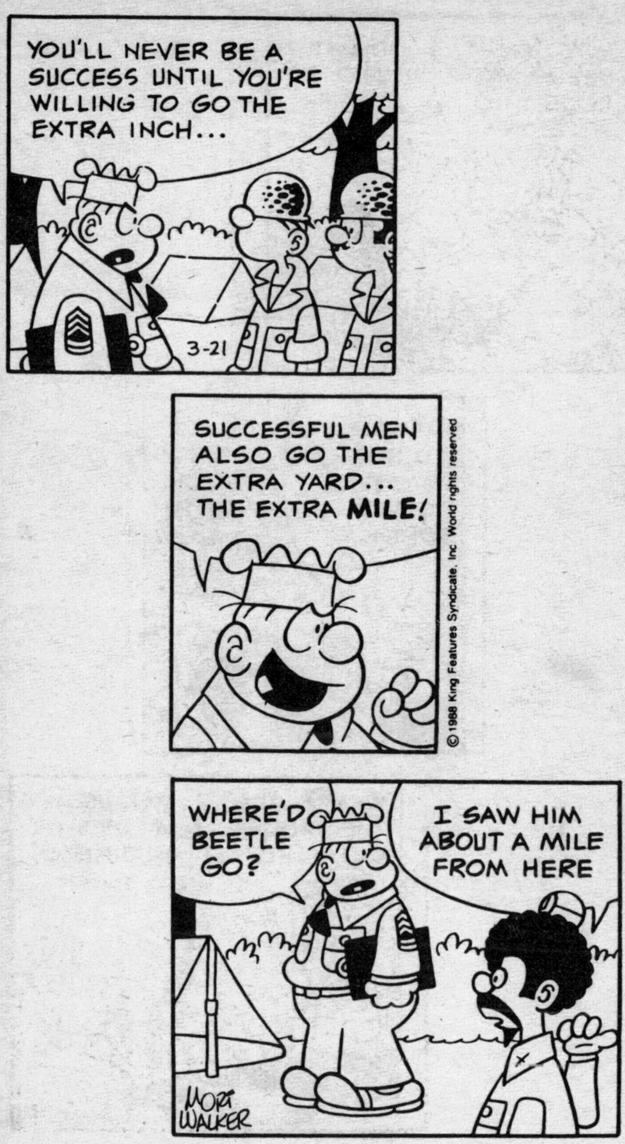
YOU'LL NEVER BE A SUCCESS UNTIL YOU'RE WILLING TO GO THE EXTRA INCH...
3-21
SUCCESSFUL MEN ALSO GO THE EXTRA YARD... THE EXTRA **MILE**!
WHERE'D BEETLE GO?
I SAW HIM ABOUT A MILE FROM HERE
MORT WALKER

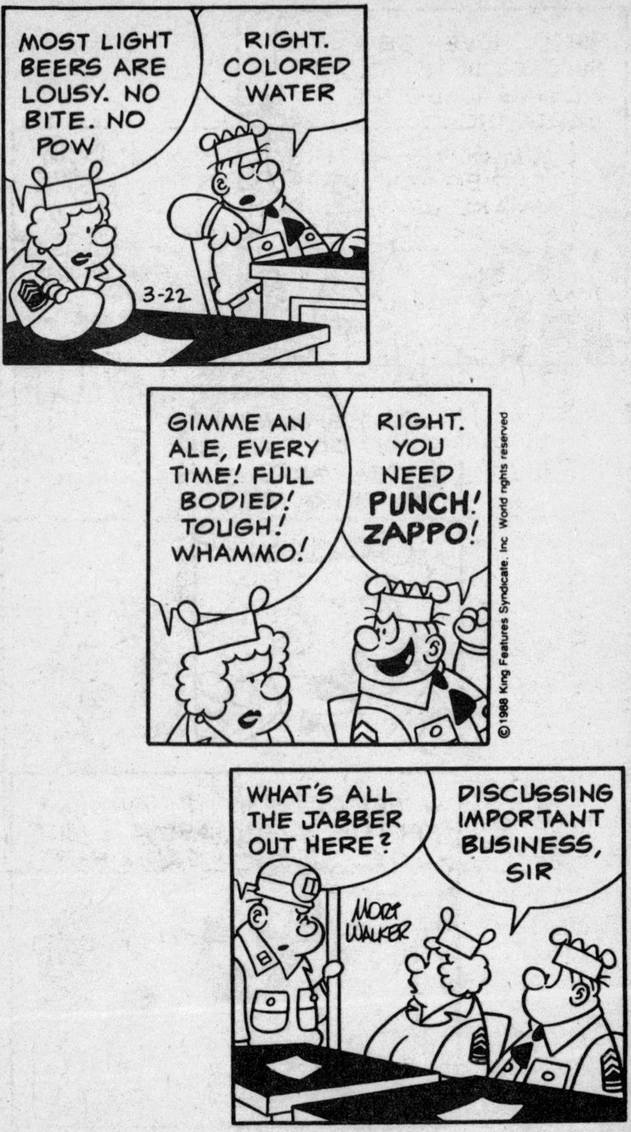
MOST LIGHT BEERS ARE LOUSY. NO BITE. NO POW
RIGHT. COLORED WATER
3-22
GIMME AN ALE, EVERY TIME! FULL BODIED! TOUGH! WHAMMO!
RIGHT. YOU NEED PUNCH! ZAPPO!
©1988 King Features Syndicate, Inc. World rights reserved
WHAT'S ALL THE JABBER OUT HERE?
DISCUSSING IMPORTANT BUSINESS, SIR
MORT WALKER

I'M GOING TO THE LADIES' ROOM TO MAKE UP
3-23
WHO DID SHE HAVE A FIGHT WITH ?
MORT WALKER

3-24
GET A RAG! SARGE JUST KNOCKED OVER HIS COFFEE
NO RUSH... IT STOPPED
MORT WALKER

WHERE ARE YOU GOING WITH SARGE'S JEEP, BEETLE?
HE WANTS ME TO TAKE IT TO THE SHOP, SIR
3-25
the DO-Nut Shop
A DOZEN ASSORTED, PLEASE
MORT WALKER

THE SMITHSONIAN HAS ARCHIE BUNKER'S CHAIR... ALAN ALDA'S GIN MILL...
3-26
© 1988 King Features Syndicate, Inc. World rights reserved
WHY NOT BEETLE BAILEY'S BED?
Z
MORT WALKER

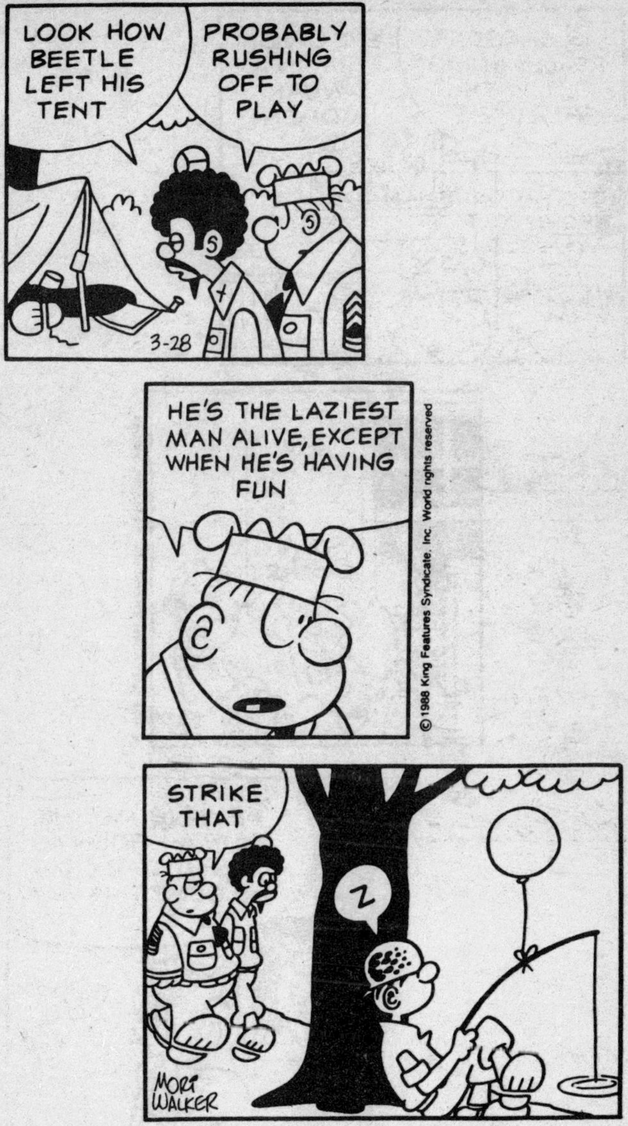
LOOK HOW BEETLE LEFT HIS TENT
PROBABLY RUSHING OFF TO PLAY
3-28
HE'S THE LAZIEST MAN ALIVE, EXCEPT WHEN HE'S HAVING FUN
© 1988 King Features Syndicate, Inc. World rights reserved
STRIKE THAT
Z
MORT WALKER

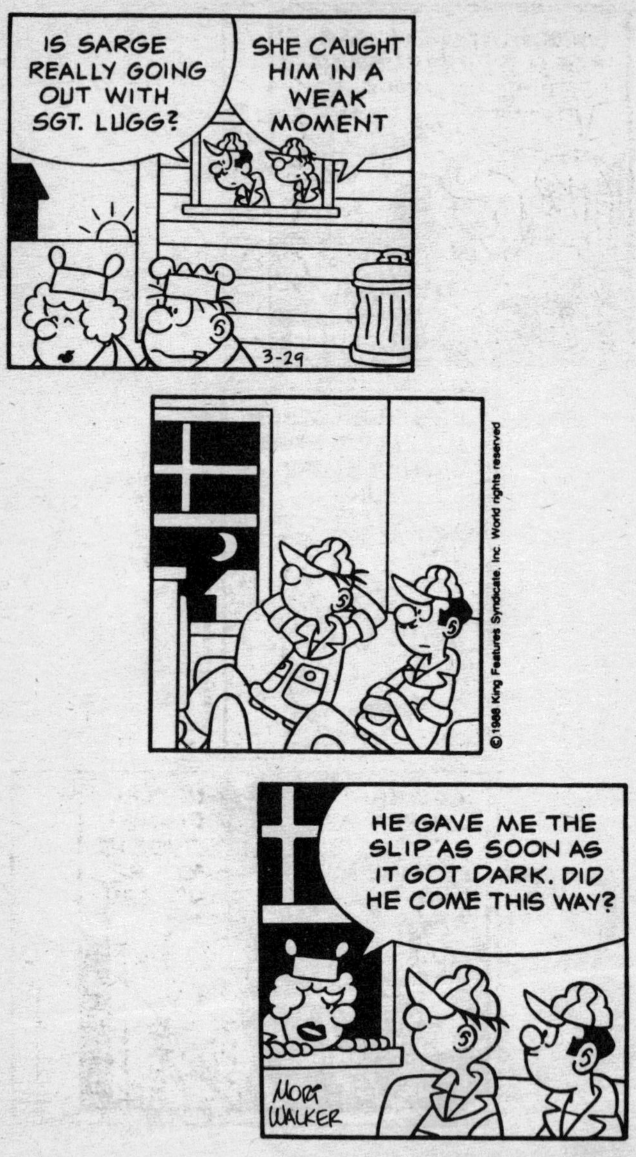
IS SARGE REALLY GOING OUT WITH SGT. LUGG?
SHE CAUGHT HIM IN A WEAK MOMENT
3-29
HE GAVE ME THE SLIP AS SOON AS IT GOT DARK. DID HE COME THIS WAY?
MORT WALKER

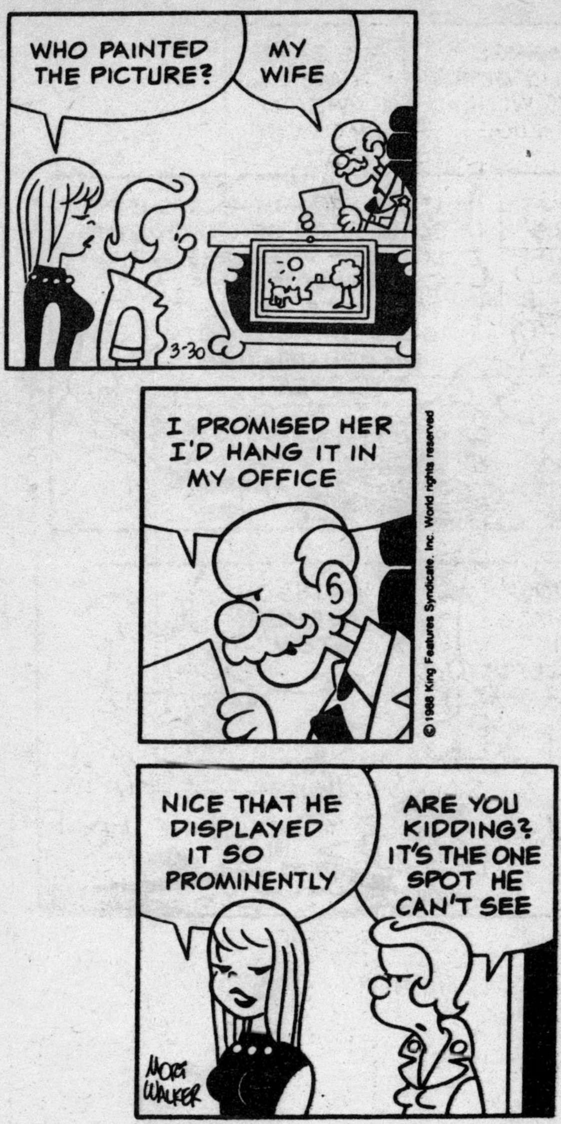
WHO PAINTED THE PICTURE?
MY WIFE
3-30
I PROMISED HER I'D HANG IT IN MY OFFICE
NICE THAT HE DISPLAYED IT SO PROMINENTLY
ARE YOU KIDDING? IT'S THE ONE SPOT HE CAN'T SEE
MORT WALKER

WHAT'S THIS STUFF ?
IT'S A VITAMIN-ENRICHED COLLECTION OF INGREDIENTS, LOVINGLY PREPARED BY A MASTER CHEF TO EXCITE THE TASTE BUDS OF THE MOST DISCRIMINATING EPICUREAN
WOW! WHAT'S IT CALLED ?
"MADISON AVENUE STEW"
MORT WALKER
3-31

IT'S EASY. JUST CLOSE YOUR EYES AND JUMP, JULIUS!
OKAY
4-1
I MEAN, OUT THERE!
MORT WALKER

I'M GOING TO TELL SARGE NOBODY CAN SLEEP ON THESE ROCKS!
4-2
IT WON'T DO YOU ANY GOOD
Z Z Z
MORT WALKER

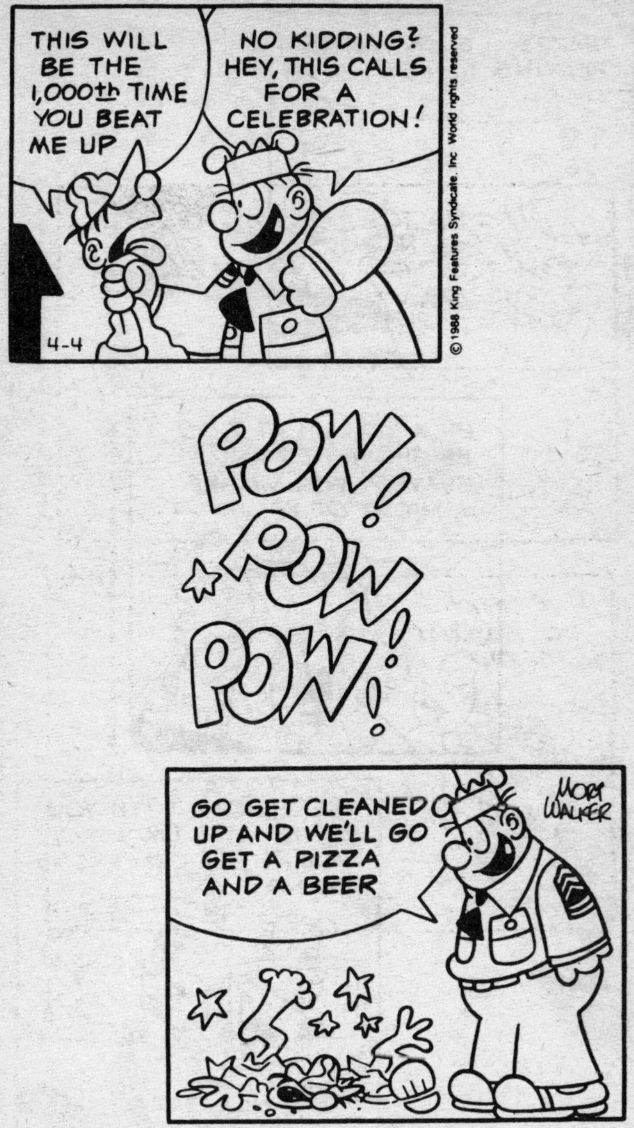
THIS WILL BE THE 1,000th TIME YOU BEAT ME UP
NO KIDDING? HEY, THIS CALLS FOR A CELEBRATION!
4-4
©1988 King Features Syndicate, Inc. World rights reserved
POW! POW! POW!
GO GET CLEANED UP AND WE'LL GO GET A PIZZA AND A BEER
MORT WALKER

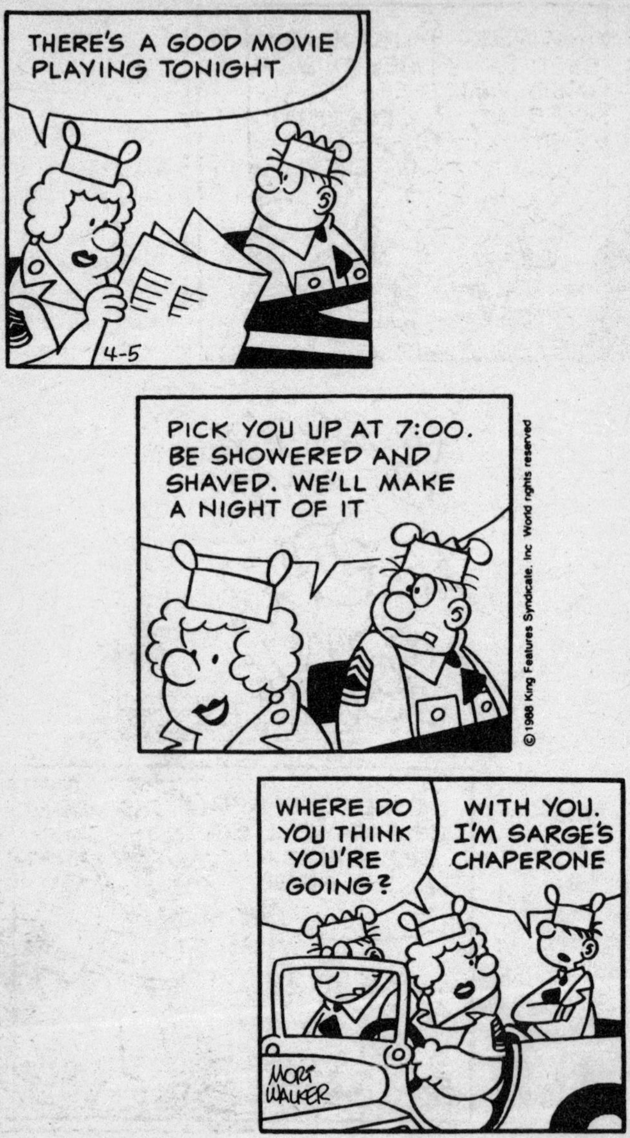
THERE'S A GOOD MOVIE PLAYING TONIGHT
4-5
PICK YOU UP AT 7:00. BE SHOWERED AND SHAVED. WE'LL MAKE A NIGHT OF IT
WHERE DO YOU THINK YOU'RE GOING?
WITH YOU. I'M SARGE'S CHAPERONE
MORT WALKER

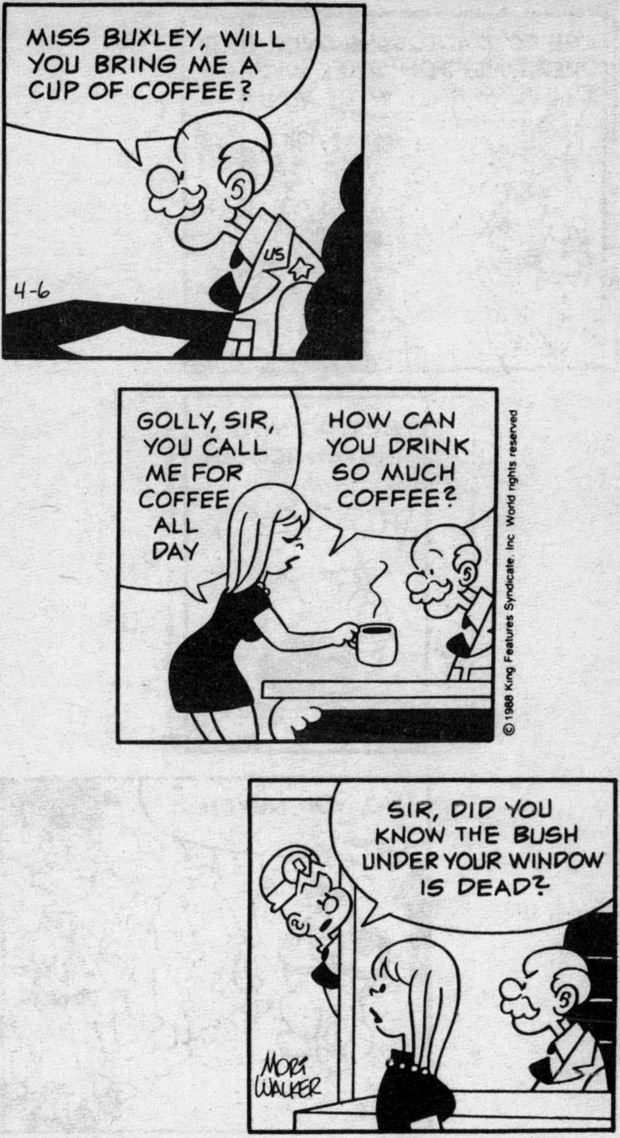
MISS BUXLEY, WILL YOU BRING ME A CUP OF COFFEE?
4-6
GOLLY, SIR, YOU CALL ME FOR COFFEE ALL DAY
HOW CAN YOU DRINK SO MUCH COFFEE?
SIR, DID YOU KNOW THE BUSH UNDER YOUR WINDOW IS DEAD?
MORT WALKER

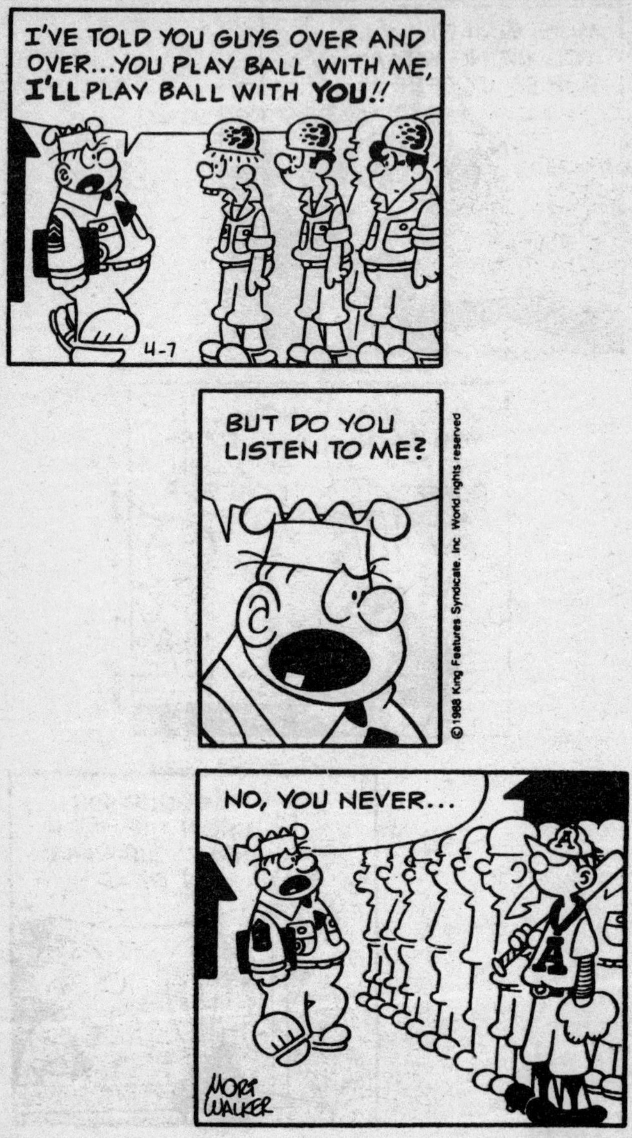
I'VE TOLD YOU GUYS OVER AND OVER...YOU PLAY BALL WITH ME, I'LL PLAY BALL WITH YOU!!
4-7
BUT DO YOU LISTEN TO ME?
NO, YOU NEVER...
MORT WALKER

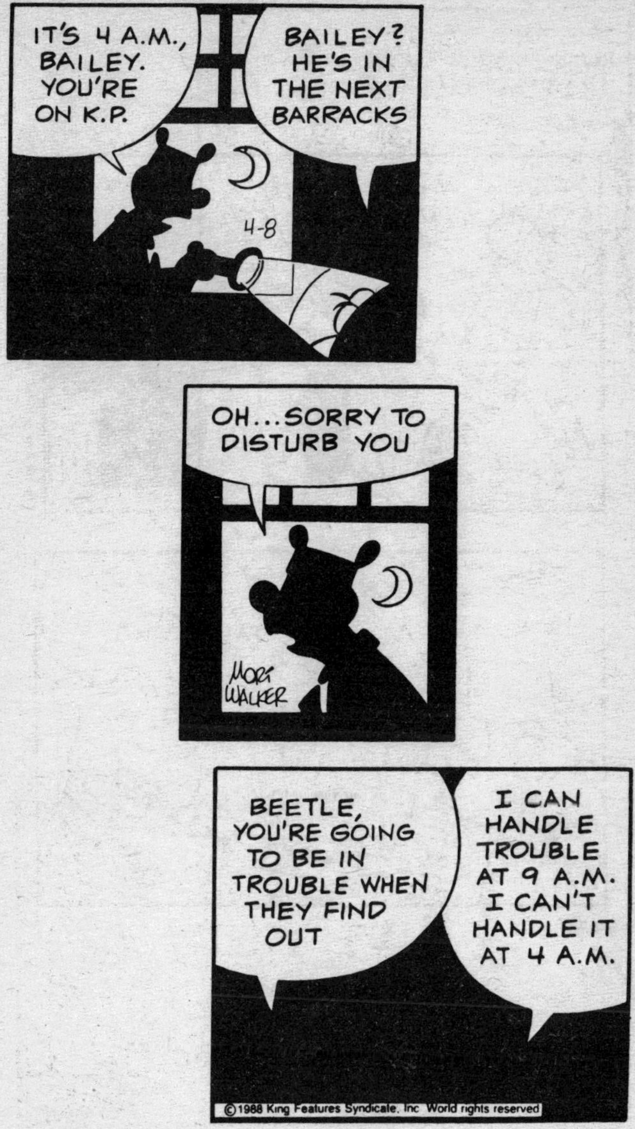
IT'S 4 A.M., BAILEY. YOU'RE ON K.P.
BAILEY? HE'S IN THE NEXT BARRACKS
4-8
OH...SORRY TO DISTURB YOU
MORT WALKER
BEETLE, YOU'RE GOING TO BE IN TROUBLE WHEN THEY FIND OUT
I CAN HANDLE TROUBLE AT 9 A.M. I CAN'T HANDLE IT AT 4 A.M.
©1988 King Features Syndicate, Inc World rights reserved

4-9
WHAT ARE YOU MAKING, SARGE?
MY KIND OF DESSERT
MORT WALKER
TA-DA STRAWBERRY TALL CAKE!

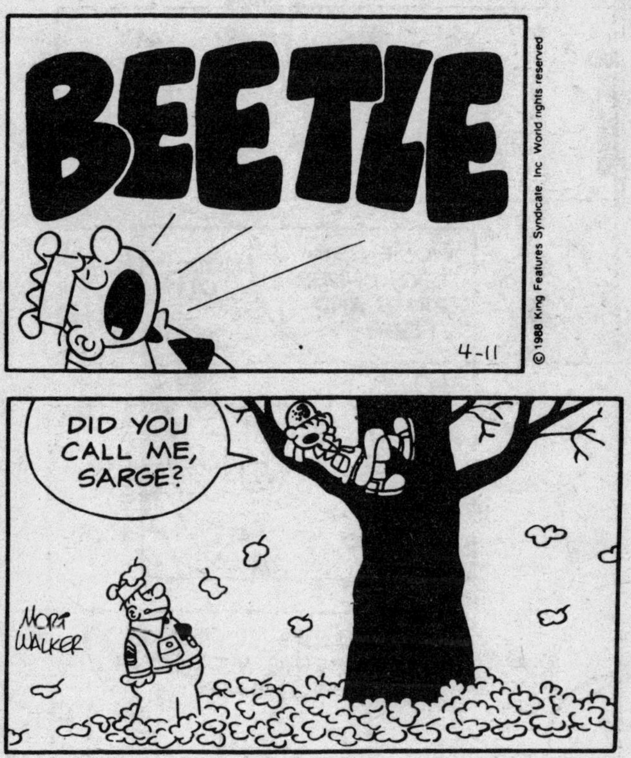
BEETLE
4-11
DID YOU CALL ME, SARGE?
MORT WALKER

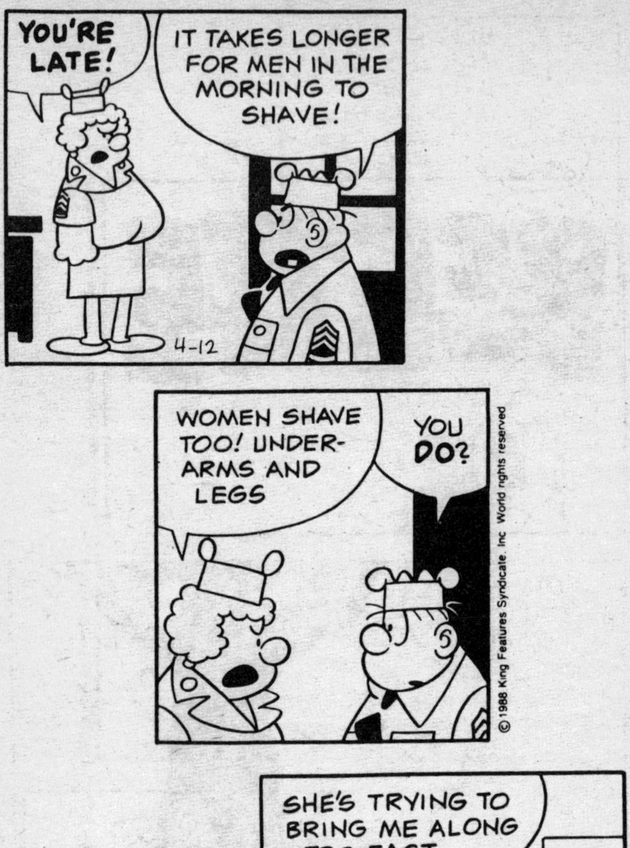
YOU'RE LATE!
IT TAKES LONGER FOR MEN IN THE MORNING TO SHAVE!
4-12
WOMEN SHAVE TOO! UNDER-ARMS AND LEGS
YOU DO?
SHE'S TRYING TO BRING ME ALONG TOO FAST
PX
MORT WALKER

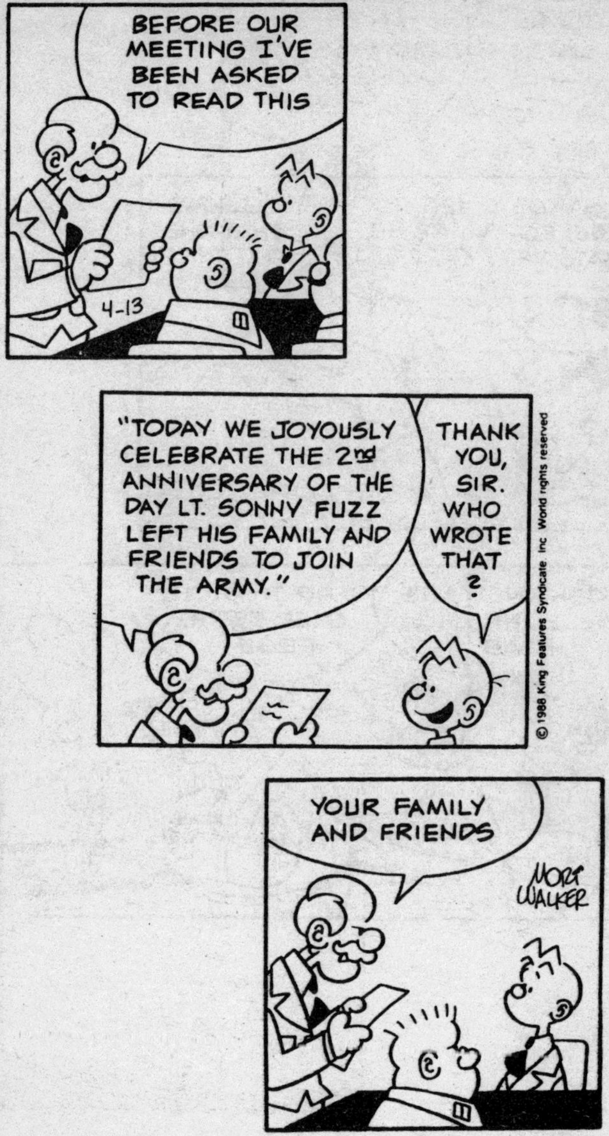
BEFORE OUR MEETING I'VE BEEN ASKED TO READ THIS
4-13
"TODAY WE JOYOUSLY CELEBRATE THE 2nd ANNIVERSARY OF THE DAY LT. SONNY FUZZ LEFT HIS FAMILY AND FRIENDS TO JOIN THE ARMY."
THANK YOU, SIR. WHO WROTE THAT?
YOUR FAMILY AND FRIENDS
MORT WALKER

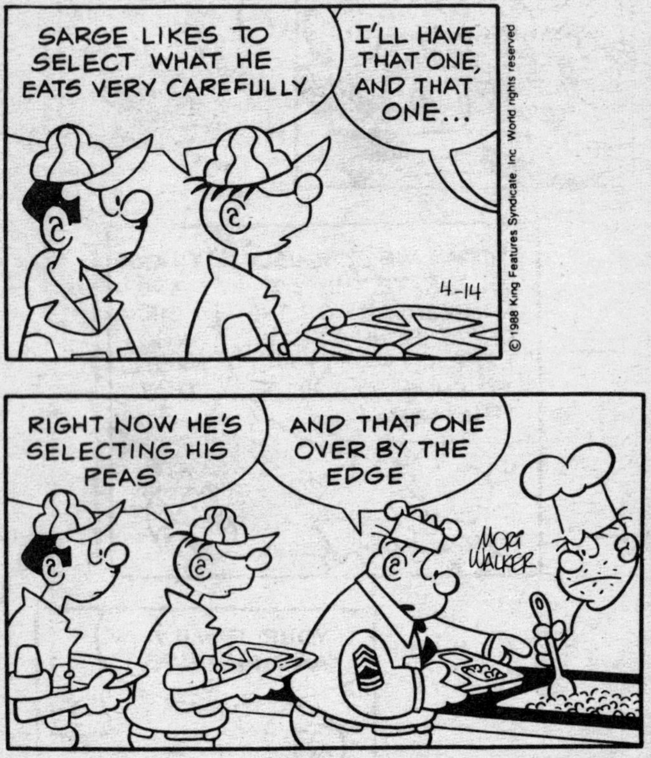
SARGE LIKES TO SELECT WHAT HE EATS VERY CAREFULLY
I'LL HAVE THAT ONE, AND THAT ONE...
4-14
RIGHT NOW HE'S SELECTING HIS PEAS
AND THAT ONE OVER BY THE EDGE
MORT WALKER

HAMERICANS MOOST LUV PEECE
DA!
MORT WALKER
YANKEE NEWS
4-15
IS PRUF HAMERICAN SOLDIER DUNT LIKE FIGHT
BEETLE BAILEY
Z
Z
LI'L BIGGER

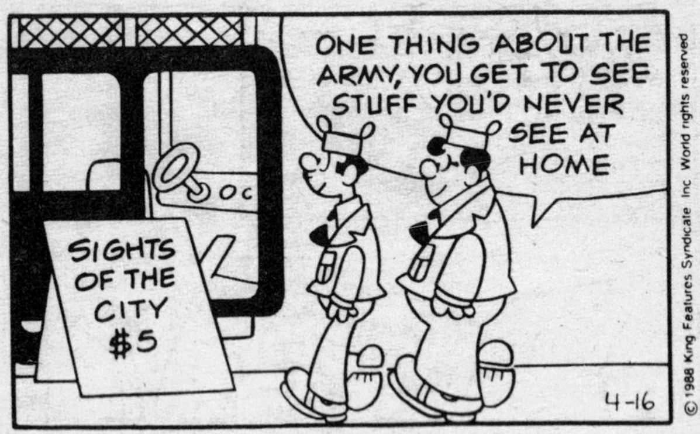
ONE THING ABOUT THE ARMY, YOU GET TO SEE STUFF YOU'D NEVER SEE AT HOME
SIGHTS OF THE CITY $5
4-16
© 1988 King Features Syndicate Inc World rights reserved

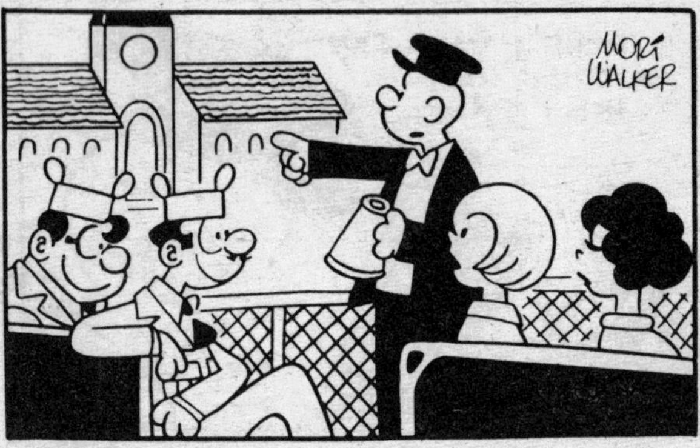
MORT WALKER

WHAT ARE YOU DOING?
THAT'S THE LAST TIME SARGE KICKS ME OUT OF BED
4-18
ARE YOU GOING TO TELL HIM OFF?
© 1988 King Features Syndicate, Inc. World rights reserved
NO
MORT WALKER

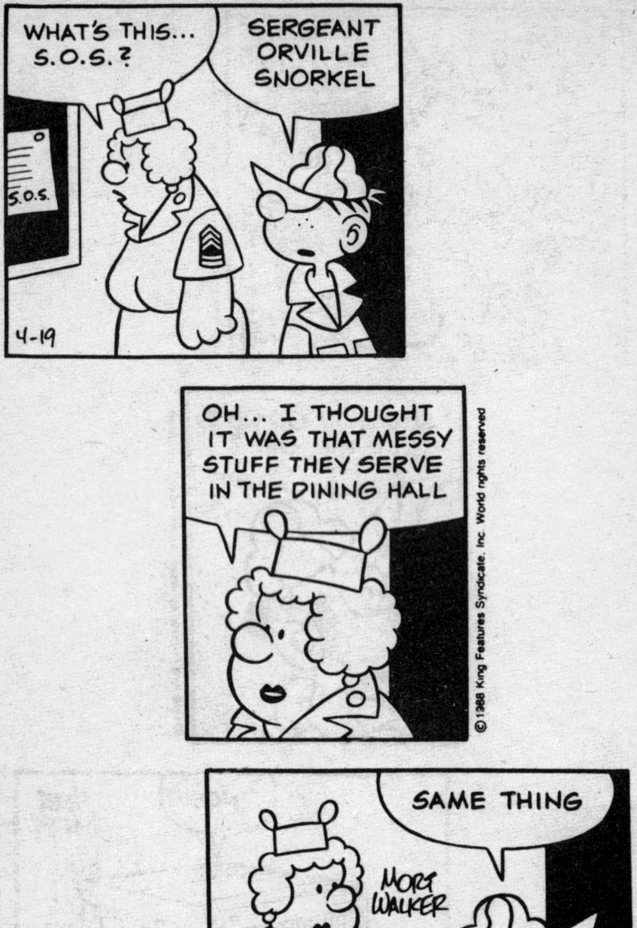
WHAT'S THIS... S.O.S.?
S.O.S.
SERGEANT ORVILLE SNORKEL
4-19
OH... I THOUGHT IT WAS THAT MESSY STUFF THEY SERVE IN THE DINING HALL
SAME THING
MORT WALKER

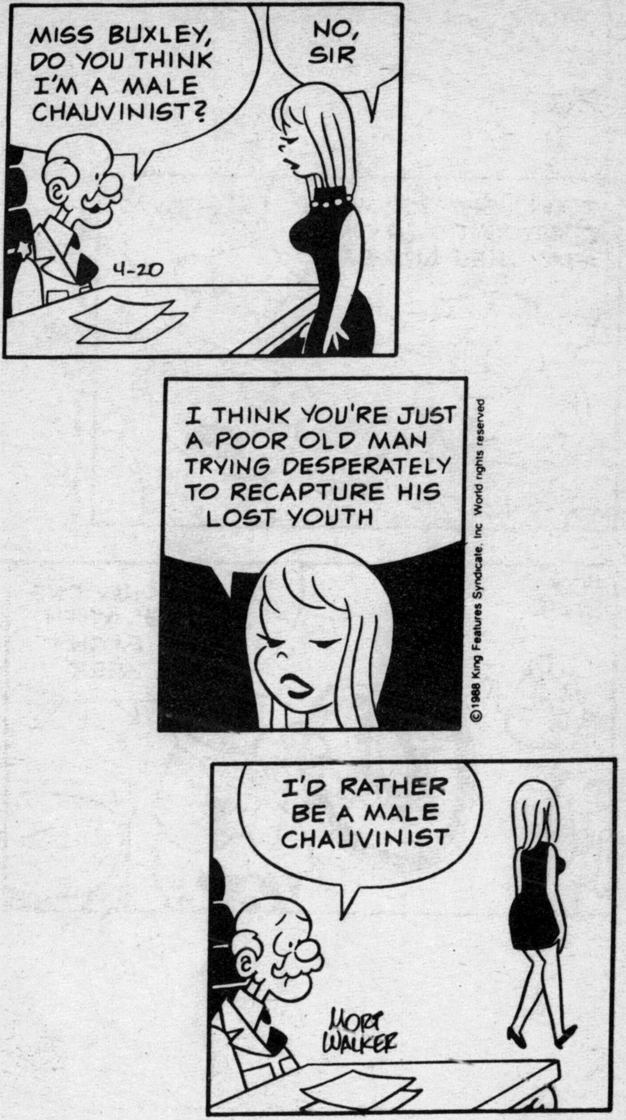
MISS BUXLEY, DO YOU THINK I'M A MALE CHAUVINIST?
NO, SIR
4-20
I THINK YOU'RE JUST A POOR OLD MAN TRYING DESPERATELY TO RECAPTURE HIS LOST YOUTH
I'D RATHER BE A MALE CHAUVINIST
MORT WALKER

I THOUGHT YOU WERE CUTTING DOWN ON STARCHES AND SALT
I AM!
4-21
©1988 King Features Syndicate, Inc World rights reserved
MORT WALKER
I HAVE ONLY ONE PRETZEL WITH EACH BEER

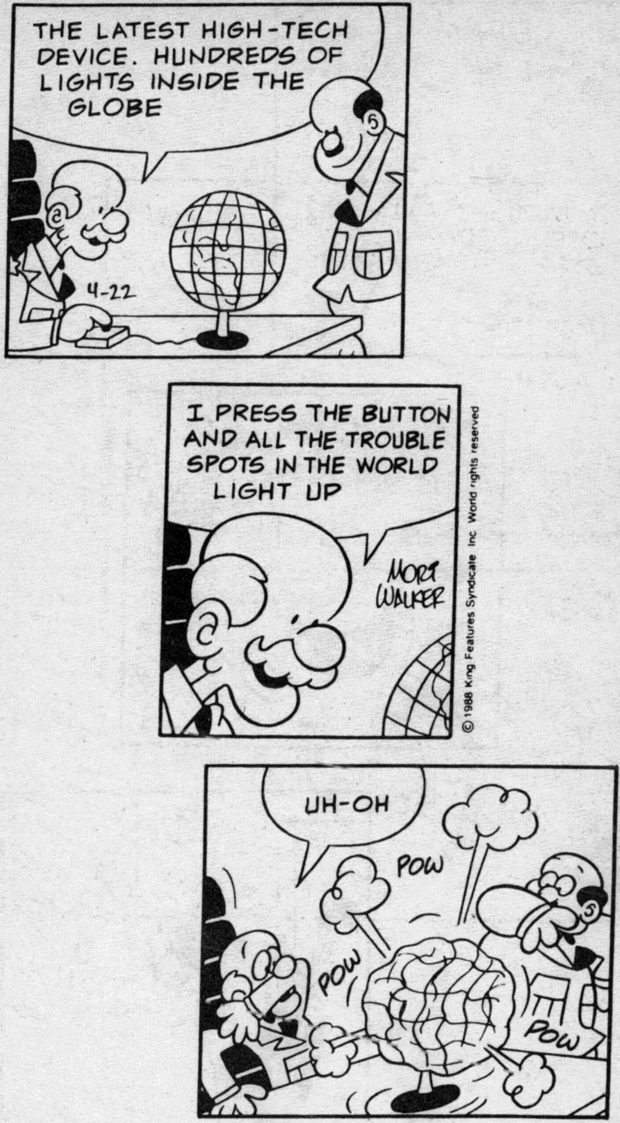
THE LATEST HIGH-TECH DEVICE. HUNDREDS OF LIGHTS INSIDE THE GLOBE
4-22
I PRESS THE BUTTON AND ALL THE TROUBLE SPOTS IN THE WORLD LIGHT UP
MORT WALKER
UH-OH
POW
POW
POW

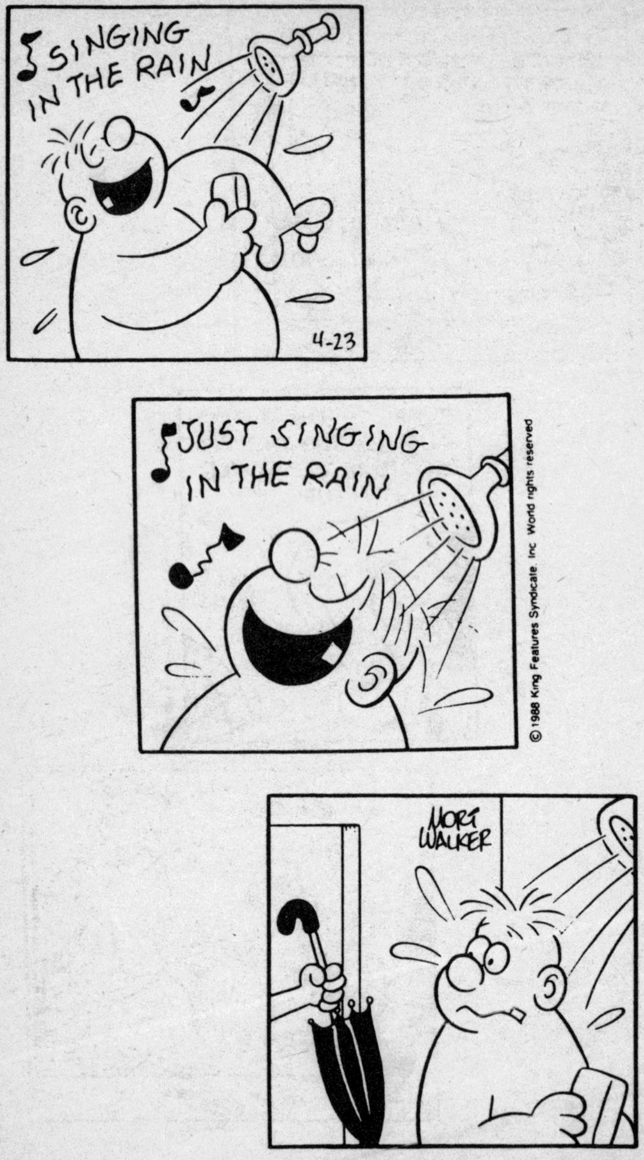
SINGING IN THE RAIN
4-23
JUST SINGING IN THE RAIN
MORT WALKER

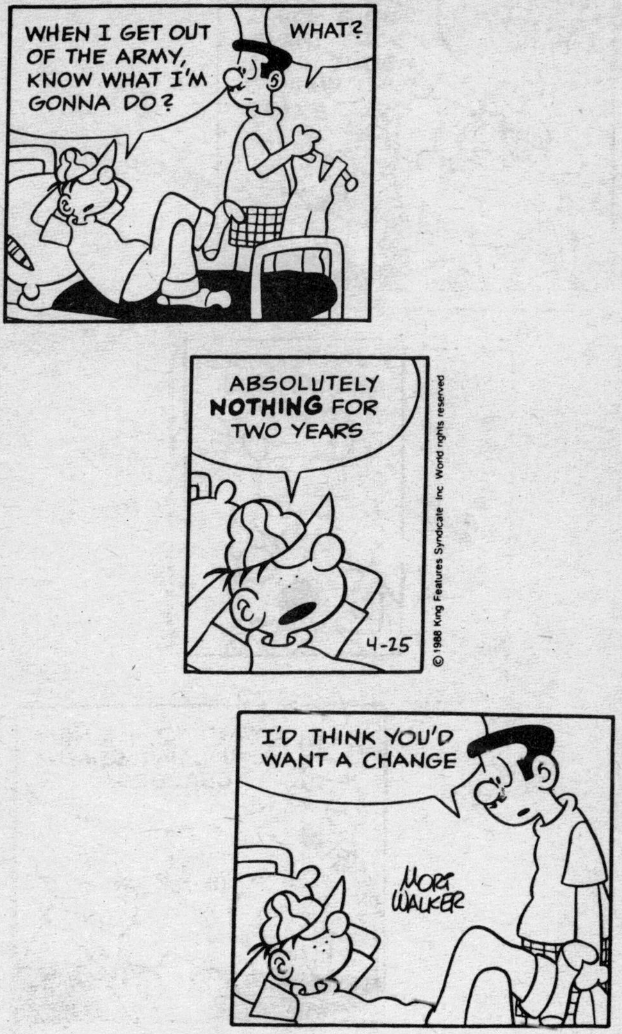
WHEN I GET OUT OF THE ARMY, KNOW WHAT I'M GONNA DO?
WHAT?
ABSOLUTELY **NOTHING** FOR TWO YEARS
4-25
I'D THINK YOU'D WANT A CHANGE
MORT WALKER

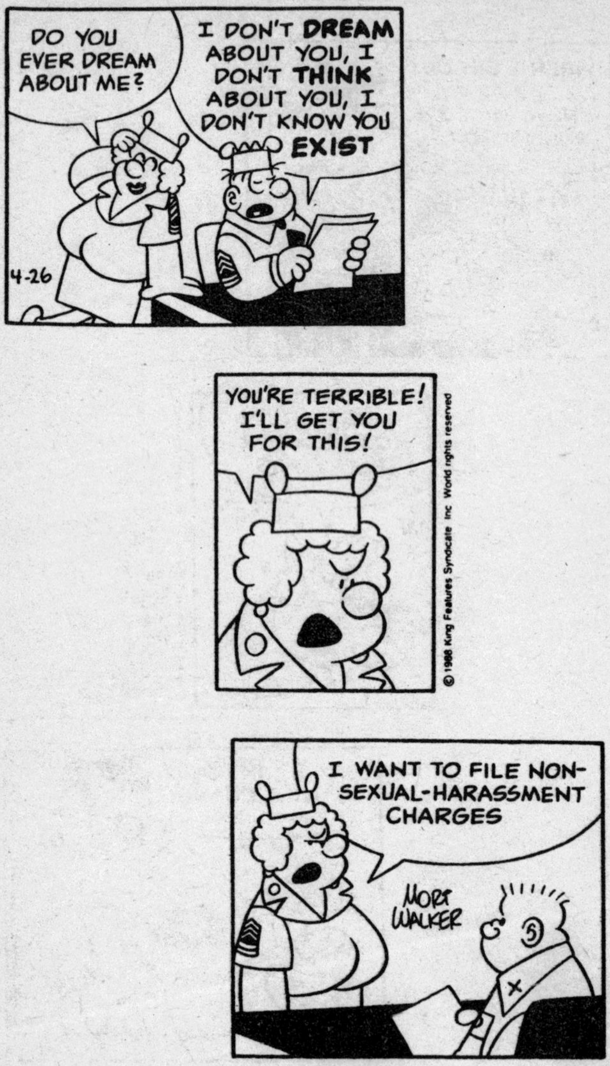
DO YOU EVER DREAM ABOUT ME?
I DON'T DREAM ABOUT YOU, I DON'T THINK ABOUT YOU, I DON'T KNOW YOU EXIST
4-26
YOU'RE TERRIBLE! I'LL GET YOU FOR THIS!
I WANT TO FILE NON-SEXUAL-HARASSMENT CHARGES
MORT WALKER

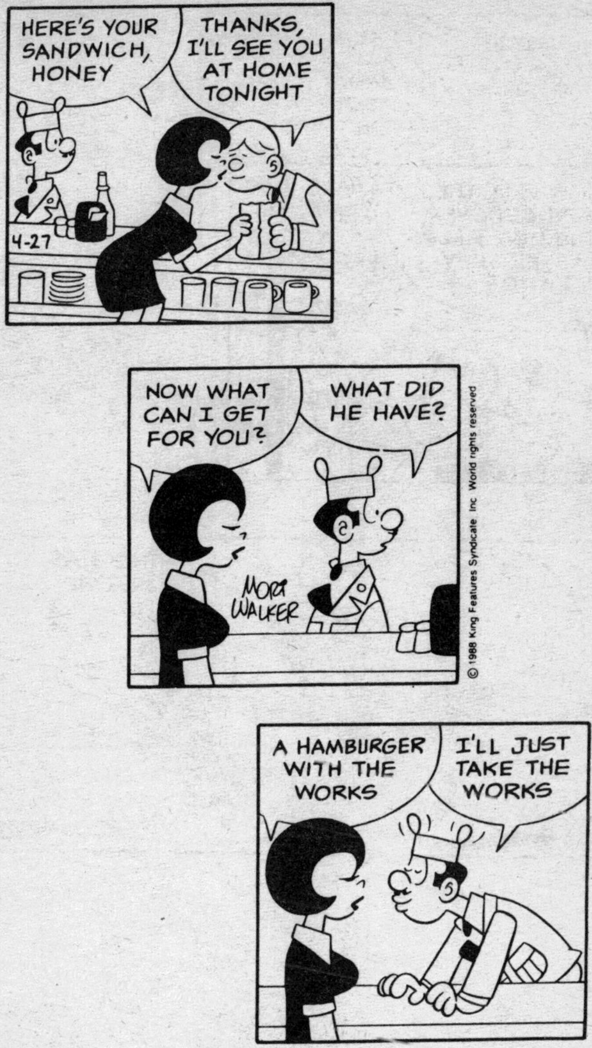
HERE'S YOUR SANDWICH, HONEY
THANKS, I'LL SEE YOU AT HOME TONIGHT
4-27
NOW WHAT CAN I GET FOR YOU?
WHAT DID HE HAVE?
MORT WALKER
A HAMBURGER WITH THE WORKS
I'LL JUST TAKE THE WORKS

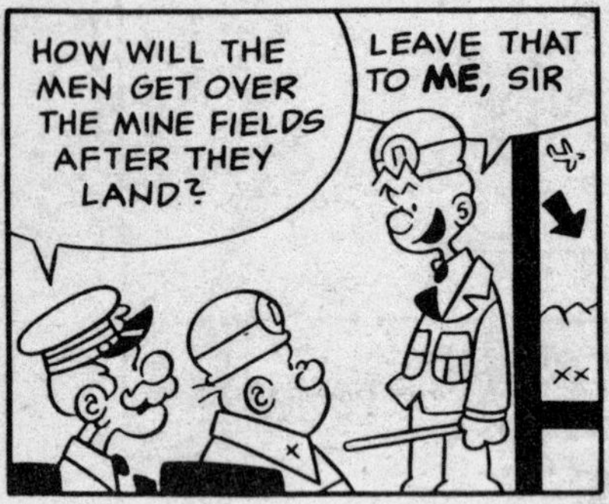
HOW WILL THE MEN GET OVER THE MINE FIELDS AFTER THEY LAND?
LEAVE THAT TO ME, SIR

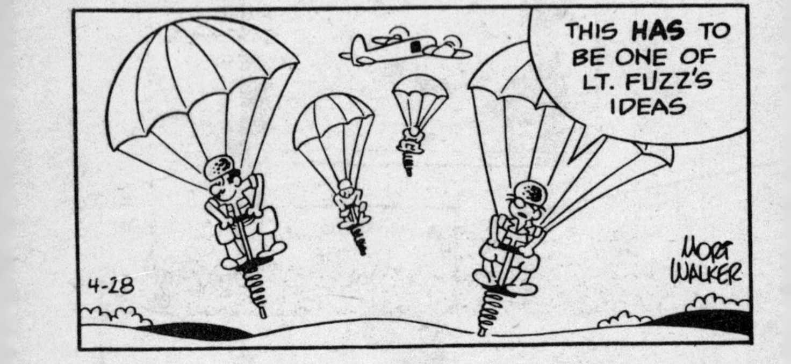
THIS HAS TO BE ONE OF LT. FUZZ'S IDEAS
4-28
MORT WALKER

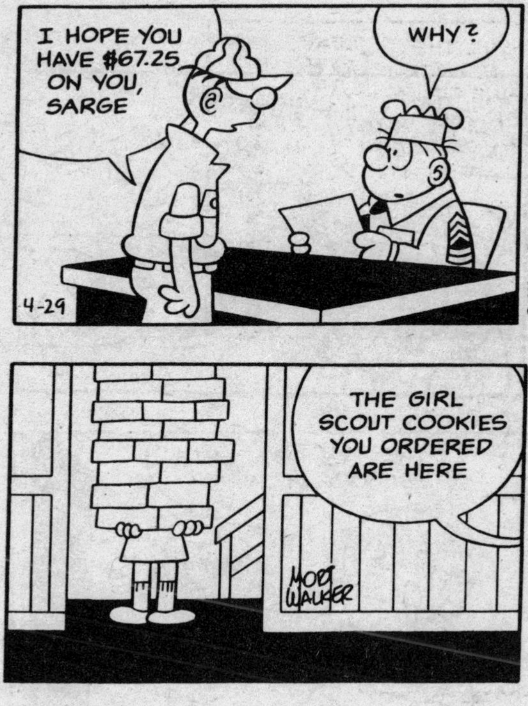
I HOPE YOU HAVE $67.25 ON YOU, SARGE
WHY?
4-29
THE GIRL SCOUT COOKIES YOU ORDERED ARE HERE
MORT WALKER

THIS TANK COMES WITH A PENTAGON WARRANTY
WHAT DOES THAT GUARANTEE?
4-30
THAT IT'S OBSOLETE BEFORE DELIVERY
MORT WALKER
© 1988 King Features Syndicate Inc World rights reserved

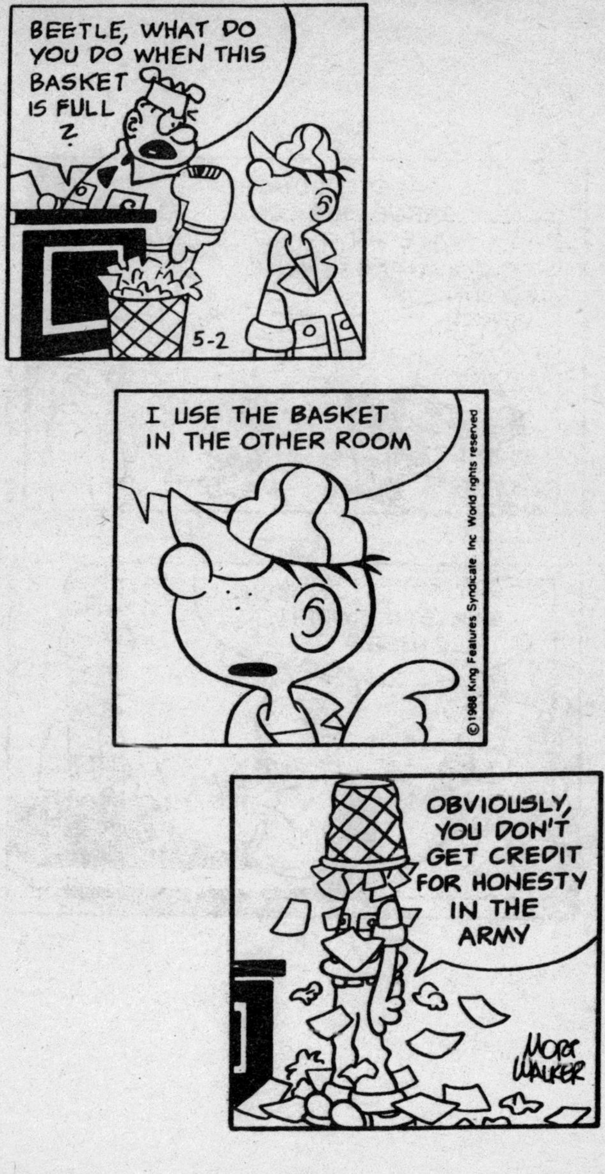
BEETLE, WHAT DO YOU DO WHEN THIS BASKET IS FULL ?
5-2
I USE THE BASKET IN THE OTHER ROOM
©1988 King Features Syndicate, Inc. World rights reserved
OBVIOUSLY, YOU DON'T GET CREDIT FOR HONESTY IN THE ARMY
MORT WALKER

I MISSED LUNCH, SARGE. DO YOU HAVE ANYTHING TO NIBBLE ON?
5-3
MORT WALKER
THAT OFFER ON YOUR EAR STILL OPEN, LOUISE?

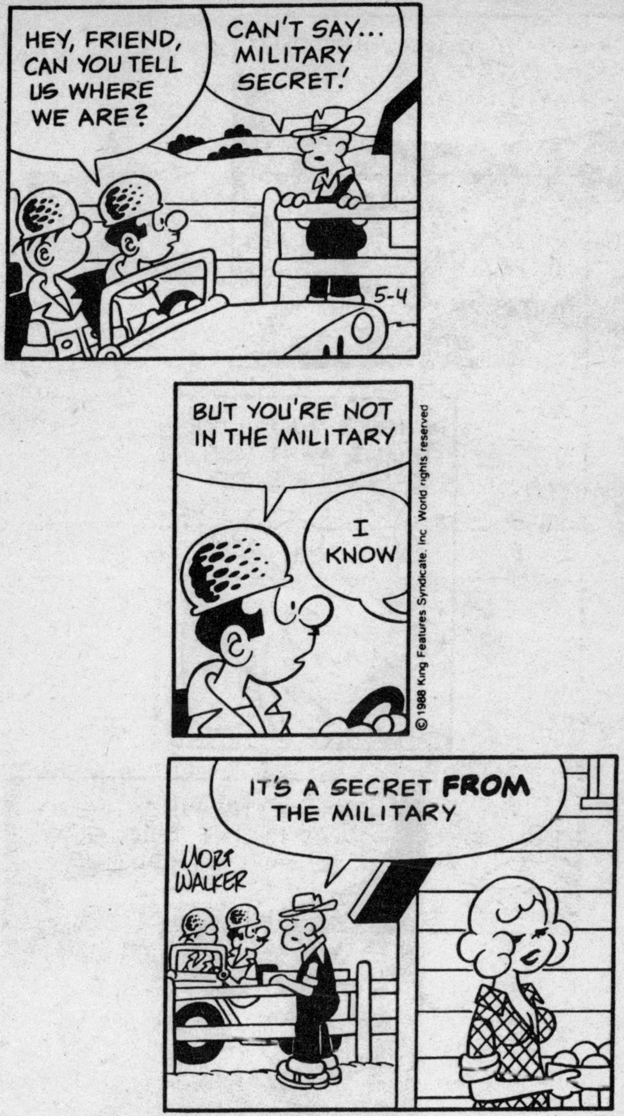
HEY, FRIEND, CAN YOU TELL US WHERE WE ARE?
CAN'T SAY... MILITARY SECRET!
5-4
BUT YOU'RE NOT IN THE MILITARY
I KNOW
IT'S A SECRET **FROM** THE MILITARY
MORT WALKER

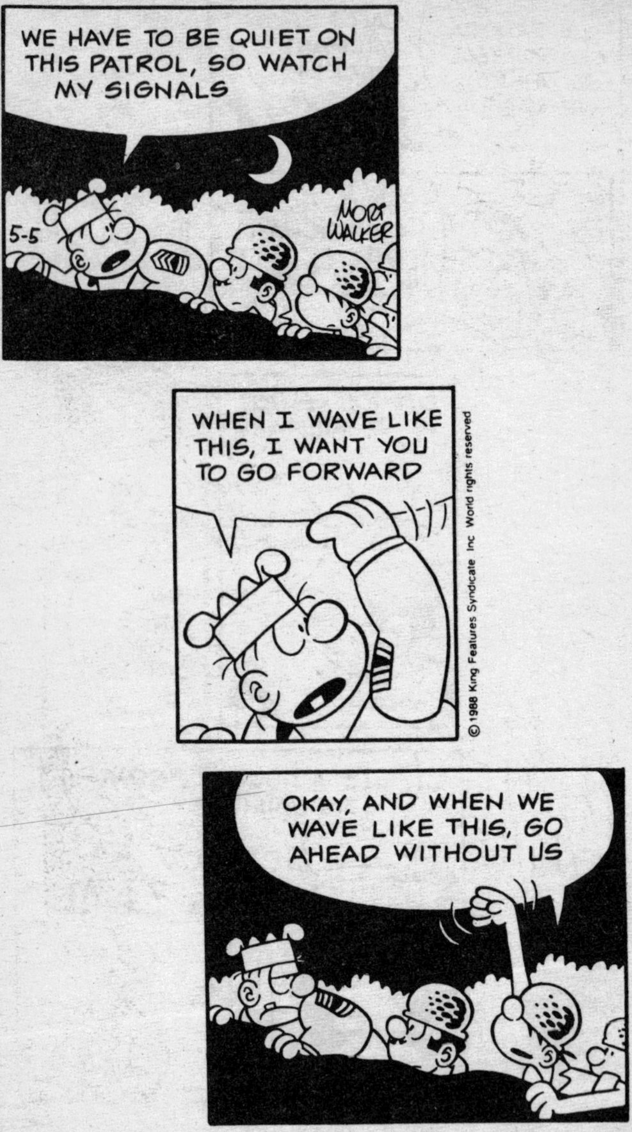
WE HAVE TO BE QUIET ON THIS PATROL, SO WATCH MY SIGNALS
5-5
MORT WALKER
WHEN I WAVE LIKE THIS, I WANT YOU TO GO FORWARD
OKAY, AND WHEN WE WAVE LIKE THIS, GO AHEAD WITHOUT US

ACCORDING TO THIS MAP THAT SHOULD BE OLD SMOKEY MOUNTAIN.
NOT ANY MORE
5-6
© 1988 King Features Syndicate, Inc. World rights reserved
MORT WALKER
SINCE IT STOPPED SMOKING, ITS NAME WAS CHANGED TO MT. HEALTHMORE

SIR, IT'S BEEN SO LONG SINCE THE MEN HAVE BEEN TO TOWN, THEY'RE CHEWING ON TENT PEGS
SORRY, NO PASSES
5-7
WELL, COULD YOU ISSUE THEM MORE TENT PEGS, THEN?
MORT WALKER

LOOKS LIKE SARGE WON'T GET BEETLE THIS TIME!
WHY NOT?
MORT WALKER
HE JUST ENTERED A SAFETY ZONE
5-9

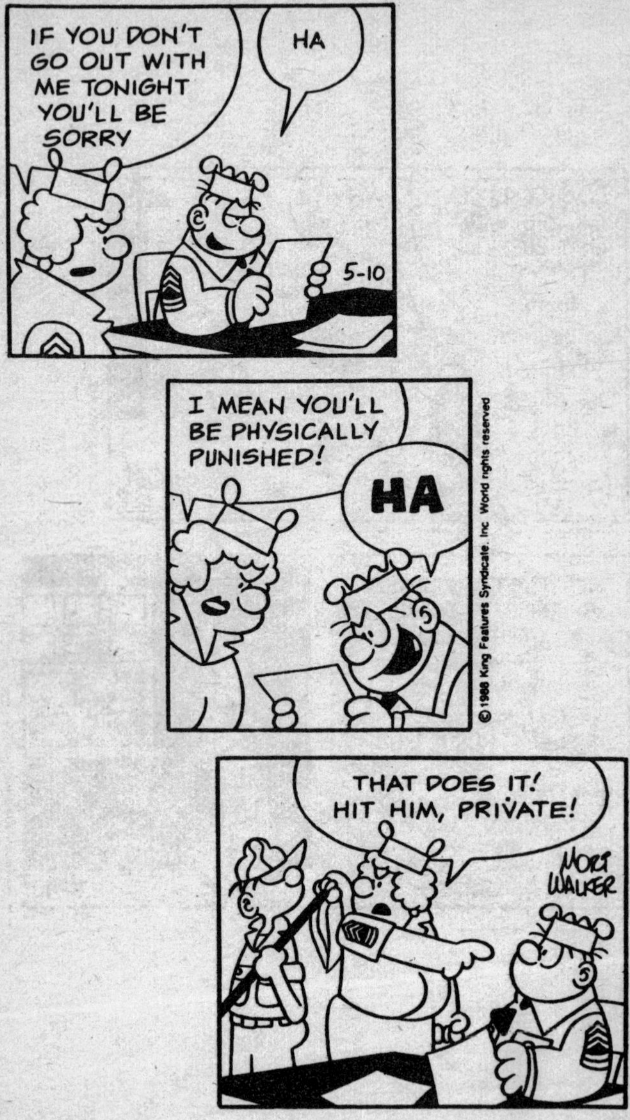
IF YOU DON'T GO OUT WITH ME TONIGHT YOU'LL BE SORRY
HA
5-10
I MEAN YOU'LL BE PHYSICALLY PUNISHED!
HA
THAT DOES IT! HIT HIM, PRIVATE!
MORT WALKER

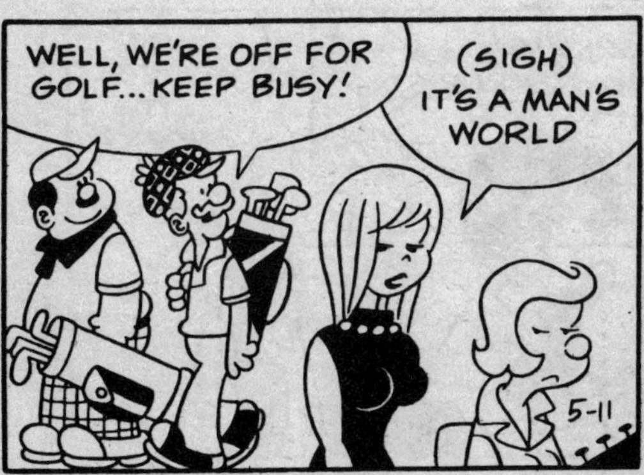
WELL, WE'RE OFF FOR GOLF... KEEP BUSY!
(SIGH) IT'S A MAN'S WORLD
5-11

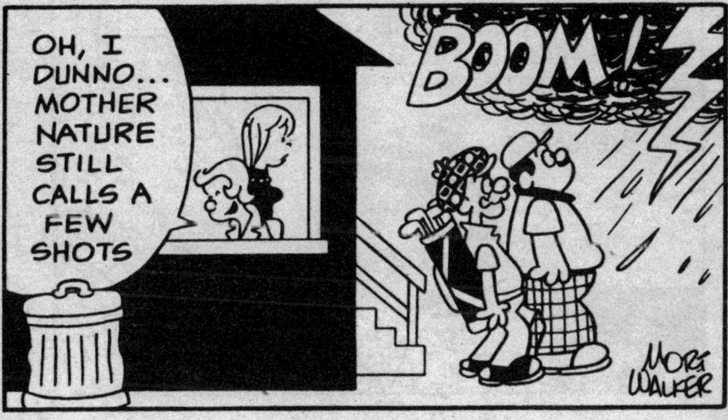
OH, I DUNNO... MOTHER NATURE STILL CALLS A FEW SHOTS
BOOM!
MORT WALKER

I'M WORKING ON A NEW ANTI-TERRORIST DEVICE
HOW DOES IT WORK?
5-12
IT SCRAMBLES THE AIRWAVES SO THE TERRORISTS CAN'T GET TV COVERAGE
MORT WALKER

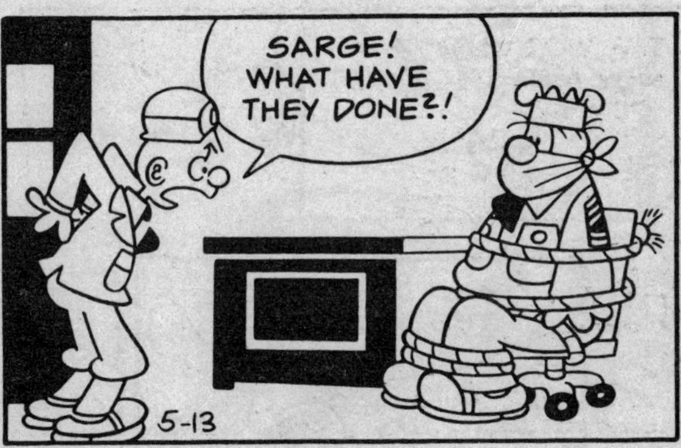
SARGE! WHAT HAVE THEY DONE?!
5-13

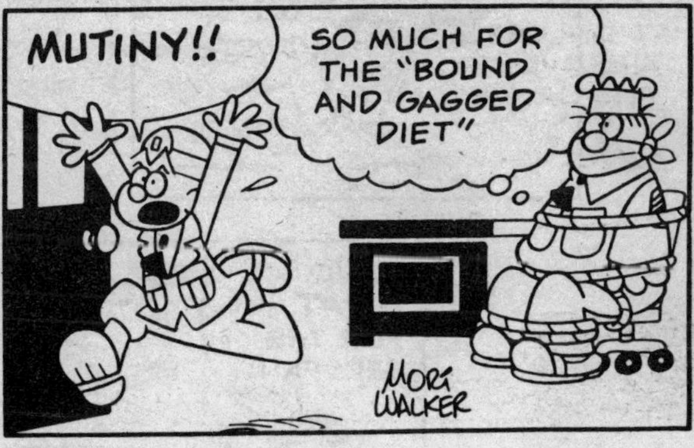
MUTINY!!
SO MUCH FOR THE "BOUND AND GAGGED DIET"
MORT WALKER

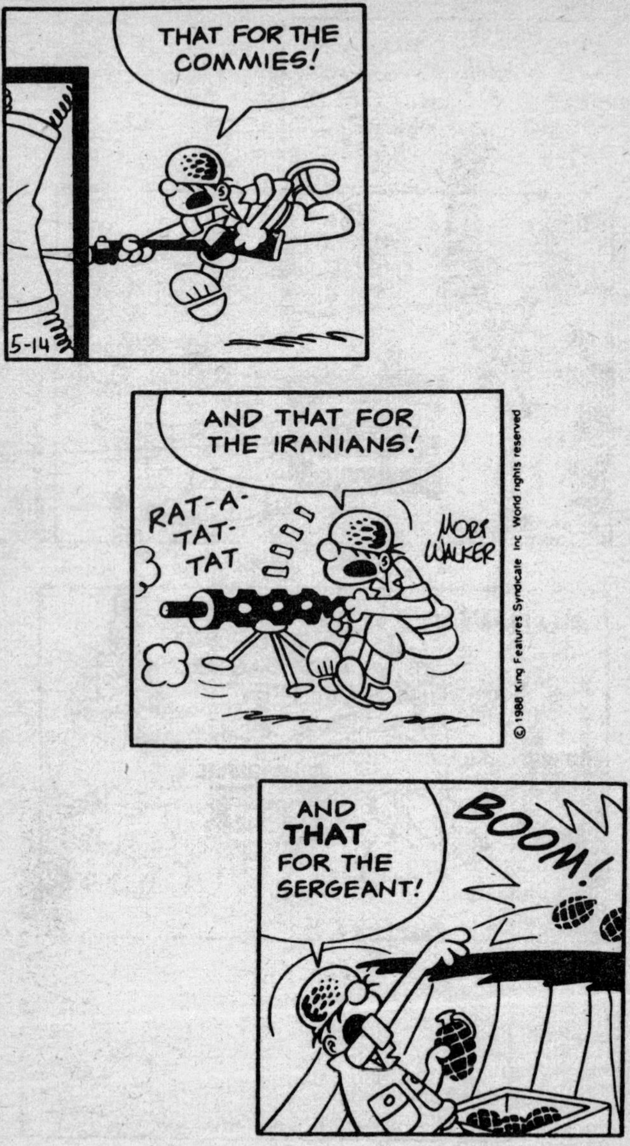
THAT FOR THE COMMIES!
5-14
AND THAT FOR THE IRANIANS!
RAT-A-TAT-TAT
MORT WALKER
AND THAT FOR THE SERGEANT!
BOOM!

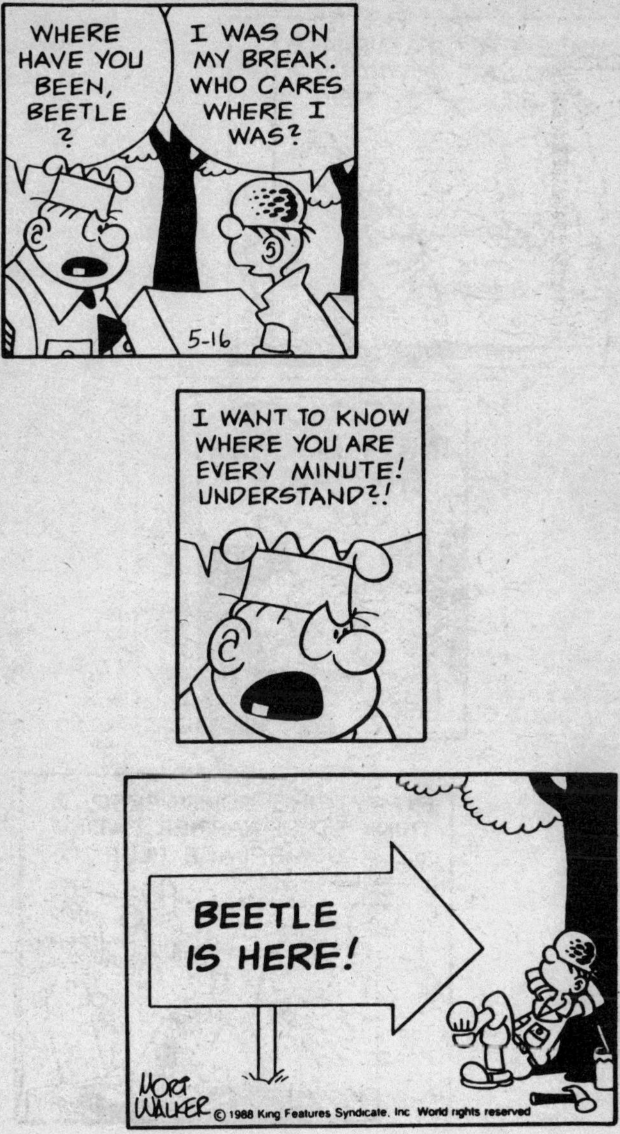
WHERE HAVE YOU BEEN, BEETLE?
I WAS ON MY BREAK. WHO CARES WHERE I WAS?
5-16
I WANT TO KNOW WHERE YOU ARE EVERY MINUTE! UNDERSTAND?!
BEETLE IS HERE!
MORT WALKER
© 1988 King Features Syndicate, Inc World rights reserved

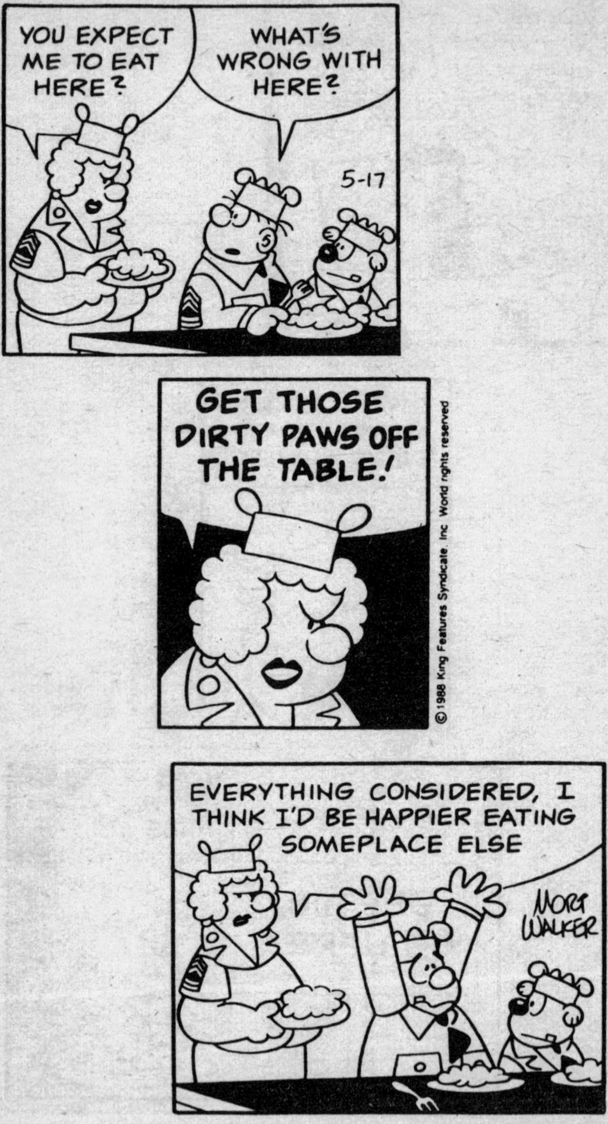

YOU EXPECT ME TO EAT HERE?
WHAT'S WRONG WITH HERE?
5-17
GET THOSE DIRTY PAWS OFF THE TABLE!
EVERYTHING CONSIDERED, I THINK I'D BE HAPPIER EATING SOMEPLACE ELSE
MORT WALKER

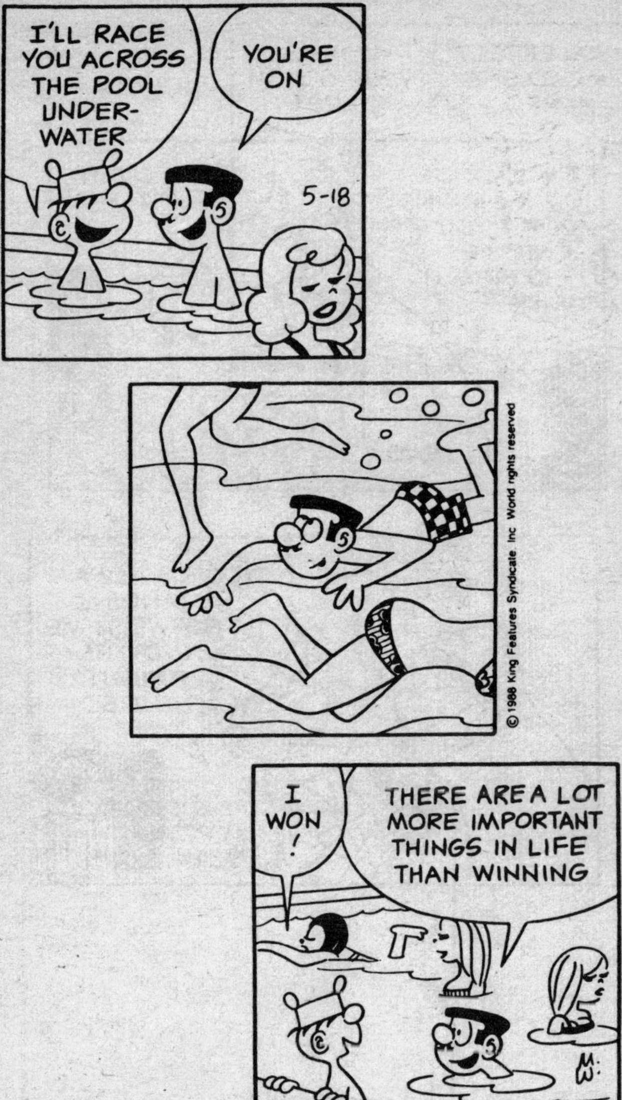
I'LL RACE YOU ACROSS THE POOL UNDER-WATER
YOU'RE ON
5-18
I WON!
THERE ARE A LOT MORE IMPORTANT THINGS IN LIFE THAN WINNING
M.W.

I'M SICK OF YOUR GRIPING! DON'T YOU EVER SEE THE BRIGHT SIDE?
MOVE OVER A LITTLE
5-19
YOU'RE ALWAYS STANDING BETWEEN ME AND THE BRIGHT SIDE
MORT WALKER

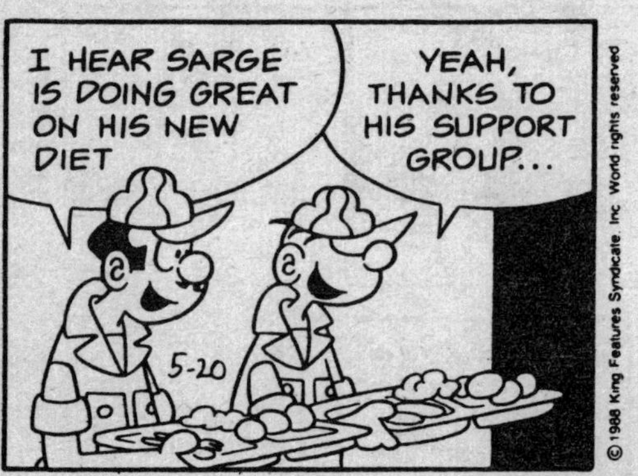
I HEAR SARGE IS DOING GREAT ON HIS NEW DIET
YEAH, THANKS TO HIS SUPPORT GROUP...
5-20
© 1988 King Features Syndicate, Inc. World rights reserved

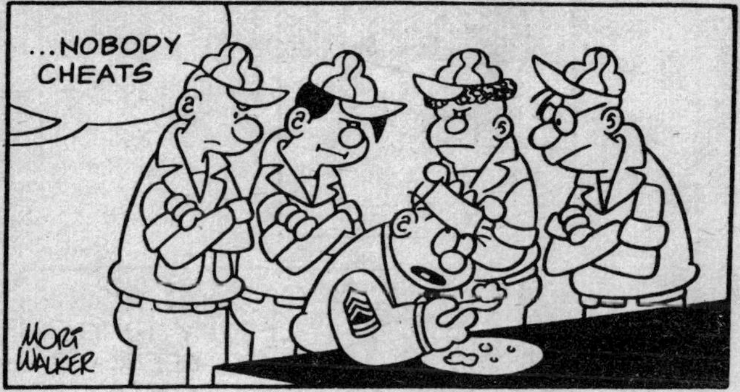
...NOBODY CHEATS
MORT WALKER

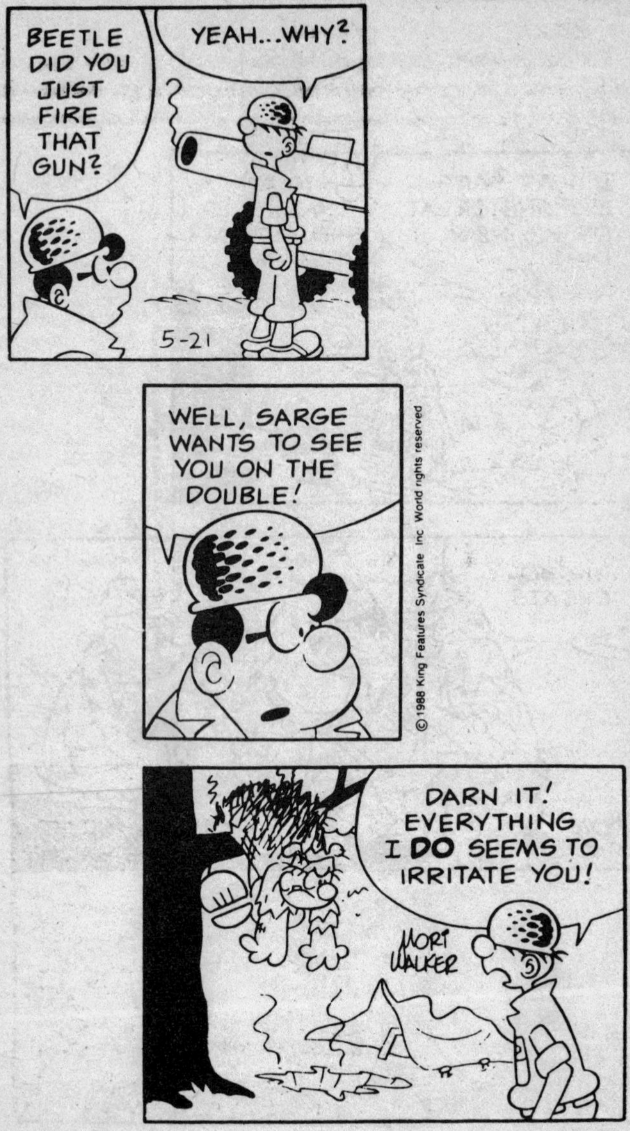
BEETLE DID YOU JUST FIRE THAT GUN?
YEAH...WHY?
5-21
WELL, SARGE WANTS TO SEE YOU ON THE DOUBLE!
DARN IT! EVERYTHING I DO SEEMS TO IRRITATE YOU!
MORT WALKER

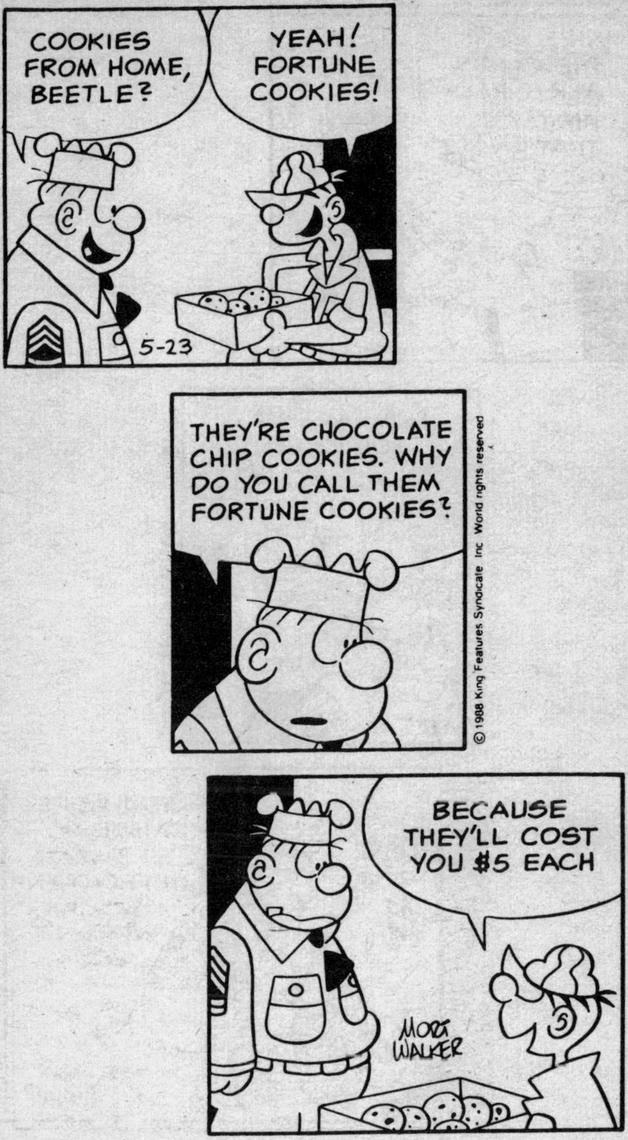
COOKIES FROM HOME, BEETLE?
YEAH! FORTUNE COOKIES!
5-23
THEY'RE CHOCOLATE CHIP COOKIES. WHY DO YOU CALL THEM FORTUNE COOKIES?
BECAUSE THEY'LL COST YOU $5 EACH
MORT WALKER

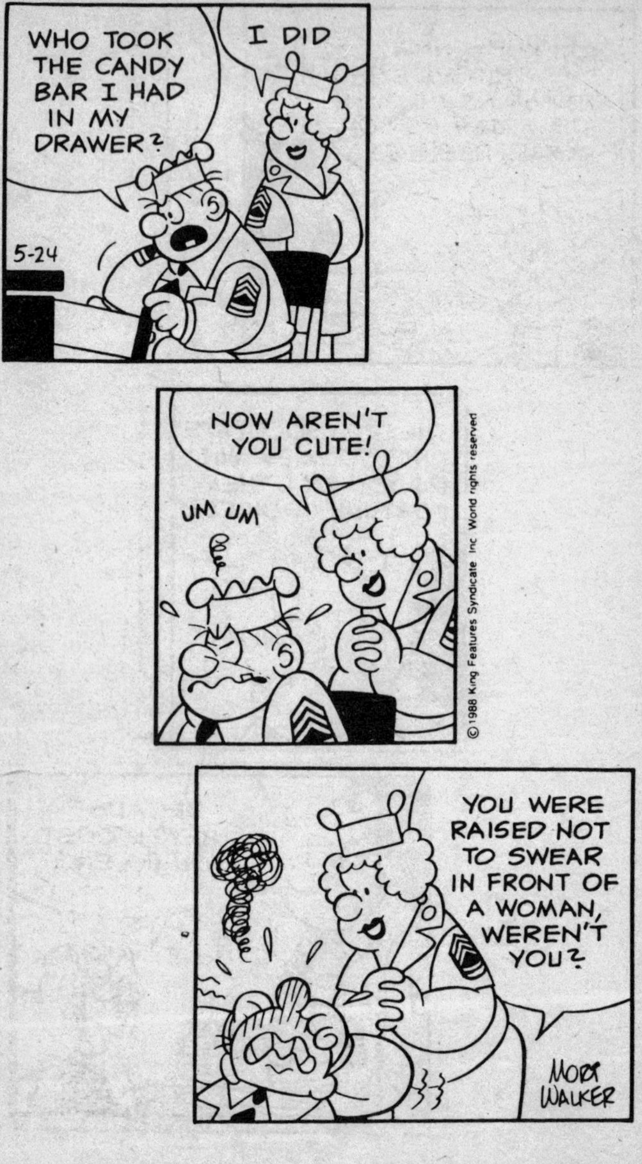
WHO TOOK THE CANDY BAR I HAD IN MY DRAWER?
I DID
5-24
NOW AREN'T YOU CUTE!
UM UM
YOU WERE RAISED NOT TO SWEAR IN FRONT OF A WOMAN, WEREN'T YOU?
MORT WALKER

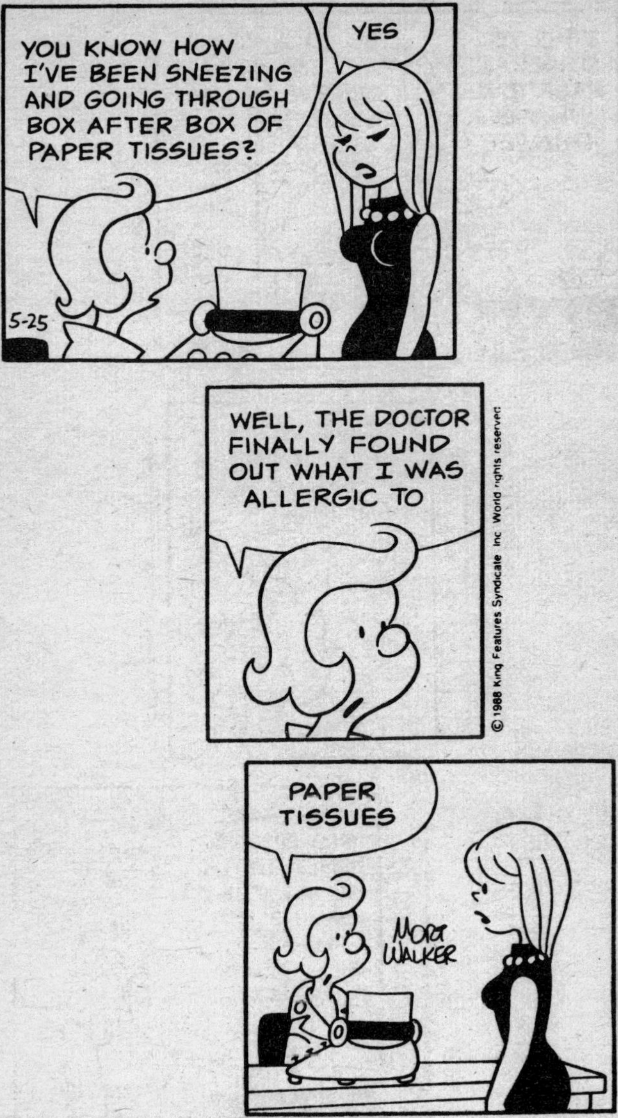
YOU KNOW HOW I'VE BEEN SNEEZING AND GOING THROUGH BOX AFTER BOX OF PAPER TISSUES?
YES
5-25
WELL, THE DOCTOR FINALLY FOUND OUT WHAT I WAS ALLERGIC TO
© 1988 King Features Syndicate Inc World rights reserved
PAPER TISSUES
MORT WALKER

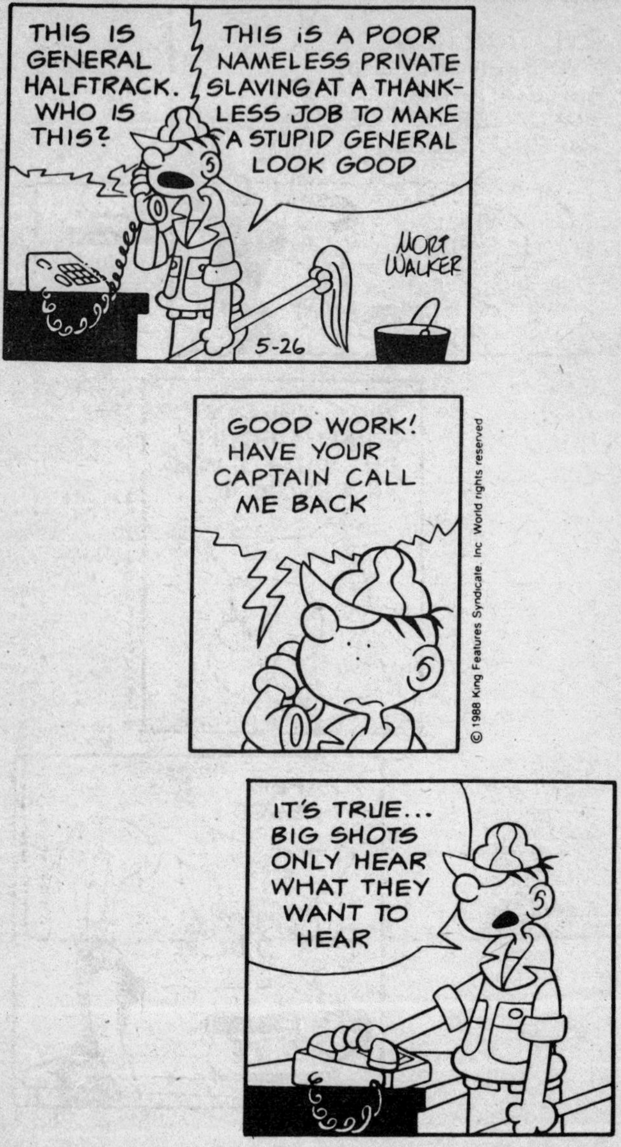
THIS IS GENERAL HALFTRACK. WHO IS THIS?
THIS iS A POOR NAMELESS PRIVATE SLAVING AT A THANK-LESS JOB TO MAKE A STUPID GENERAL LOOK GOOD
MORT WALKER
5-26
GOOD WORK! HAVE YOUR CAPTAIN CALL ME BACK
IT'S TRUE... BIG SHOTS ONLY HEAR WHAT THEY WANT TO HEAR

GAINED A LITTLE WEIGHT, SARGE?
OH, YEAH? WHADDA YOU KNOW?
5-27
I KNOW THAT GUYS WHO LOSE WEIGHT DON'T CHANGE THE KNOBS WHEN THEY GET OFF
MORT WALKER
© 1988 King Features Syndicate, Inc. World rights reserved

REMEMBER, ENLISTED MEN ALWAYS DO WHAT THEY'RE TOLD
AND OFFICERS ARE ALWAYS RIGHT
AND GENERALS ALWAYS GENERALIZE
© 1988 King Features Syndicate, Inc. World rights reserved
MORT WALKER
5-28

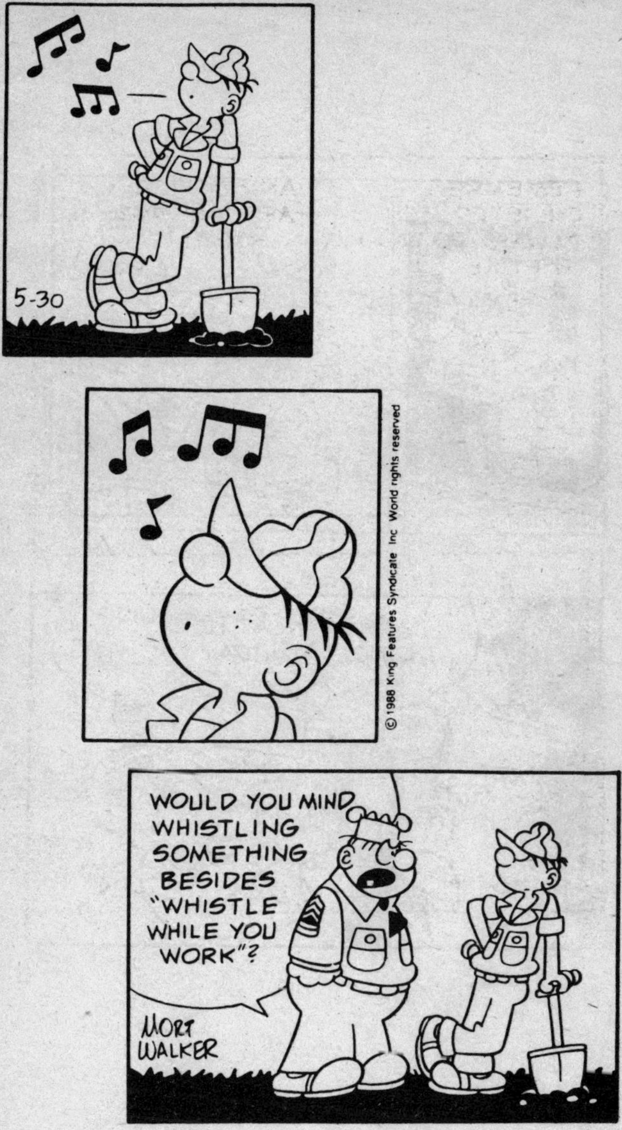
5-30
WOULD YOU MIND WHISTLING SOMETHING BESIDES "WHISTLE WHILE YOU WORK"?
MORT WALKER

FIND OUT WHO DREW THAT...
LUGG
5-31
© 1988 King Features Syndicate, Inc. World rights reserved.
...AND WHAT HE'S DOING SATURDAY NIGHT!
MORT WALKER

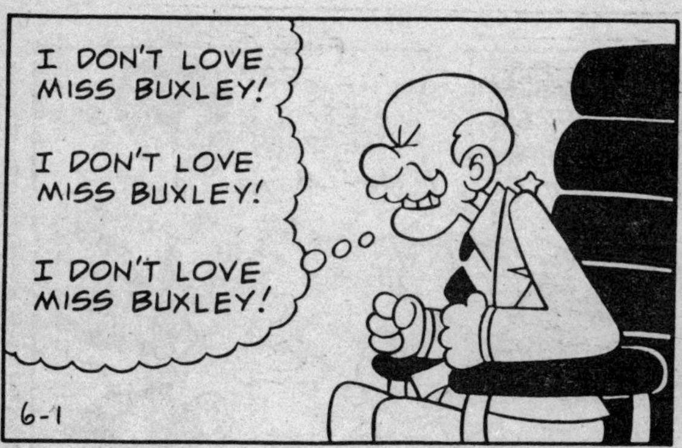
I DON'T LOVE MISS BUXLEY!
I DON'T LOVE MISS BUXLEY!
I DON'T LOVE MISS BUXLEY!
6-1

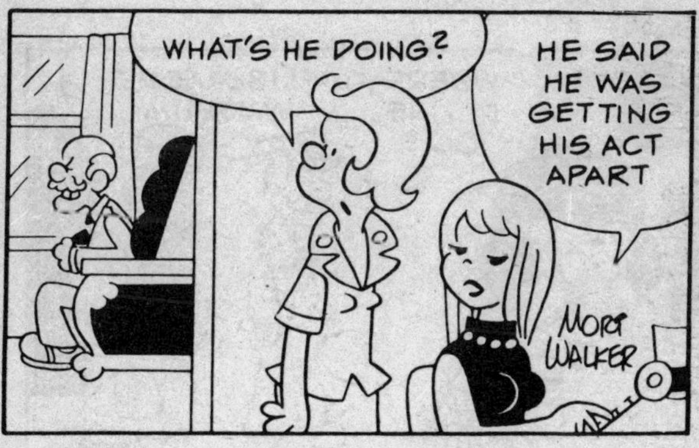
WHAT'S HE DOING?
HE SAID HE WAS GETTING HIS ACT APART
MORT WALKER

LT. FLAP CAME BACK FROM VACATION LOOKING DEPRESSED
HE MET HIS MATCH
6-2
WHERE DID HE GO?
LIBERACE'S MUSEUM
MORT WALKER

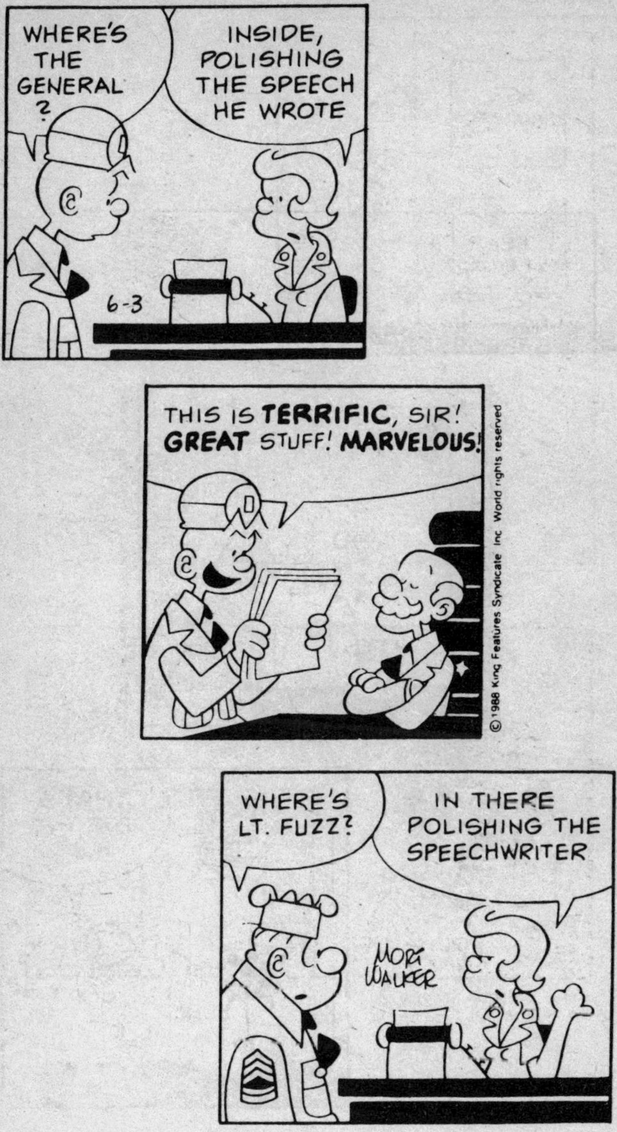
WHERE'S THE GENERAL?
INSIDE, POLISHING THE SPEECH HE WROTE
6-3
THIS IS **TERRIFIC**, SIR! **GREAT** STUFF! **MARVELOUS!**
WHERE'S LT. FUZZ?
IN THERE POLISHING THE SPEECHWRITER
MORT WALKER

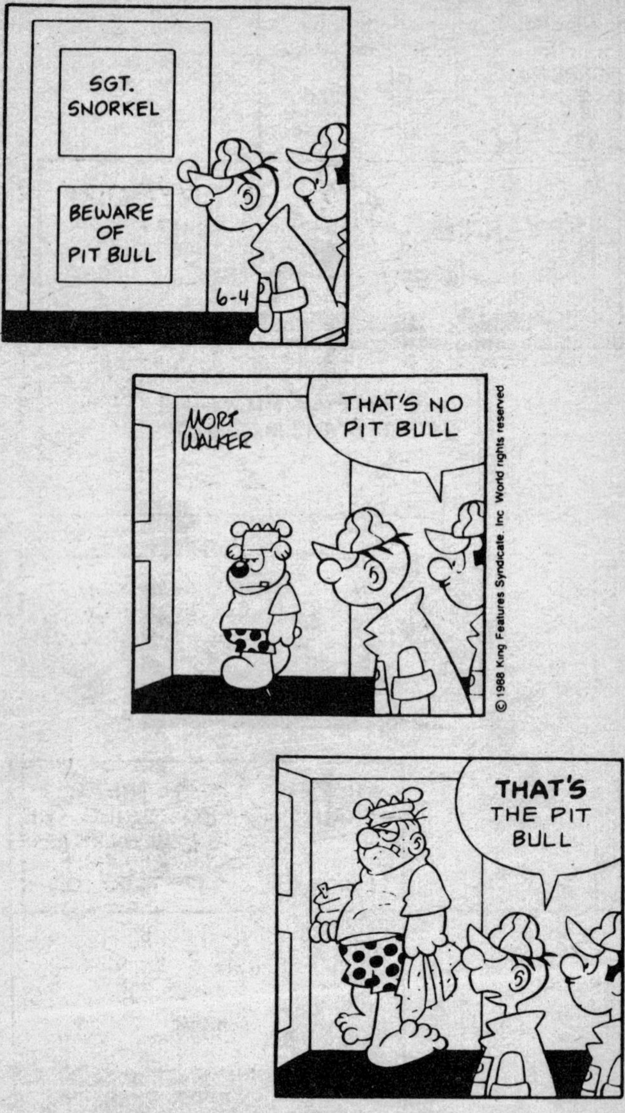
SGT. SNORKEL
BEWARE OF PIT BULL
6-4
MORT WALKER
THAT'S NO PIT BULL
THAT'S THE PIT BULL

5:30! REVEILLE!
EVERYBODY UP!
UP AND AT 'EM!
ROLL CALL IN TEN MINUTES!
MORT WALKER
6-6
QUIET! HOW CAN ANYONE SLEEP WITH ALL THAT YELLING?!

I NEVER THOUGHT LOUISE LUGG WOULD GET SARGE TO GO OUT WITH HER
6-7
© 1988 King Features Syndicate Inc World rights reserved
YOU DIDN'T KNOW HER POWER OF PERSUASION
MORT WALKER

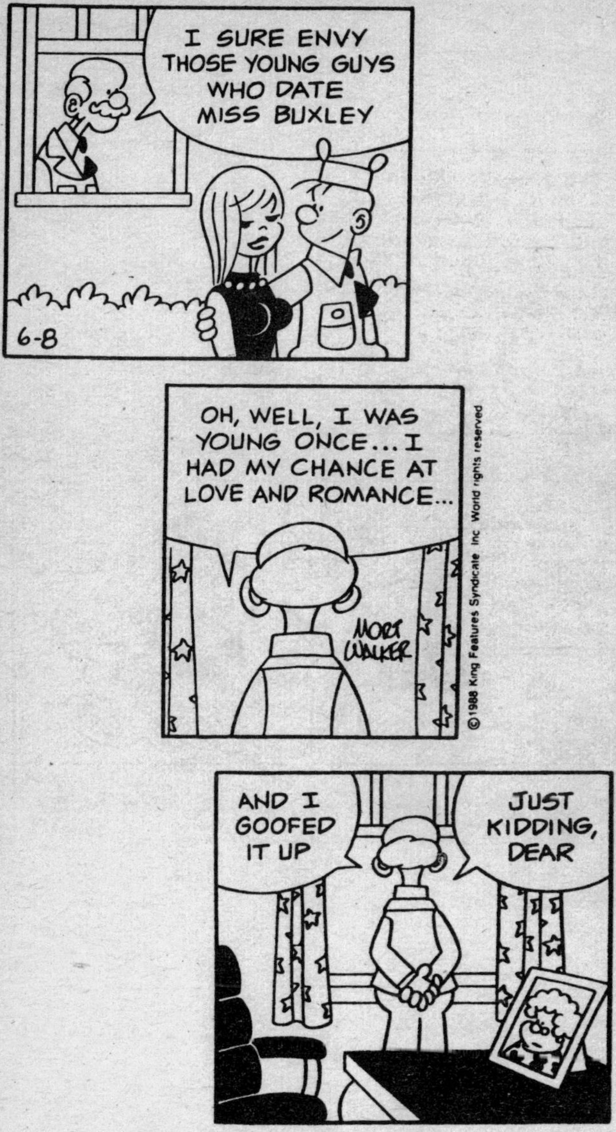
I SURE ENVY THOSE YOUNG GUYS WHO DATE MISS BUXLEY
6-8
OH, WELL, I WAS YOUNG ONCE... I HAD MY CHANCE AT LOVE AND ROMANCE...
MORT WALKER
AND I GOOFED IT UP
JUST KIDDING, DEAR

THE GENERAL ORDERED EVERYONE OVERWEIGHT TO PARTICIPATE IN THESE FIELD EVENTS
WHICH EVENT IS THIS?
6-9
THE 100-YARD WADDLE
MORT WALKER
© 1988 King Features Syndicate Inc. World rights reserved

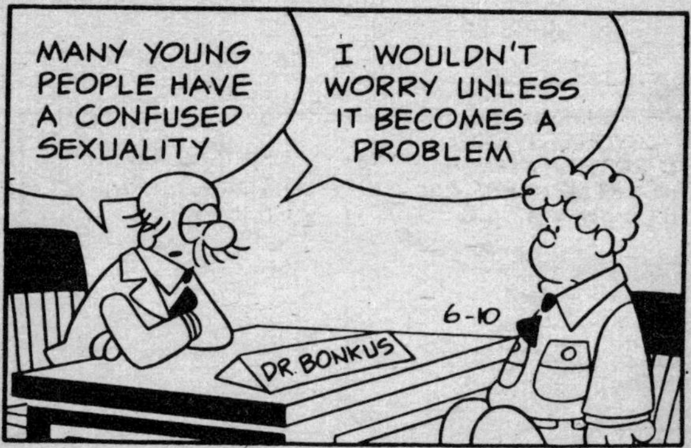
MANY YOUNG PEOPLE HAVE A CONFUSED SEXUALITY
I WOULDN'T WORRY UNLESS IT BECOMES A PROBLEM
6-10
DR. BONKUS

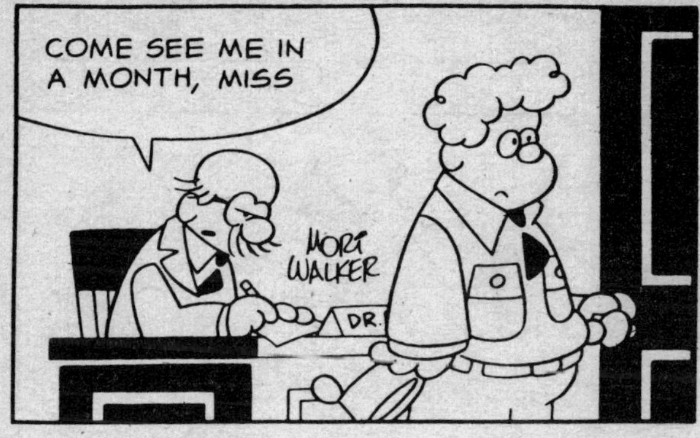
COME SEE ME IN A MONTH, MISS
MORT WALKER
DR.

WHAT DO YOU DO FOR A PAIN IN THE NECK?
HAVE YOU TRIED PUTTING LINIMENT ON IT, SIR?
6-11
© 1988 King Features Syndicate, Inc. World rights reserved
MORT WALKER

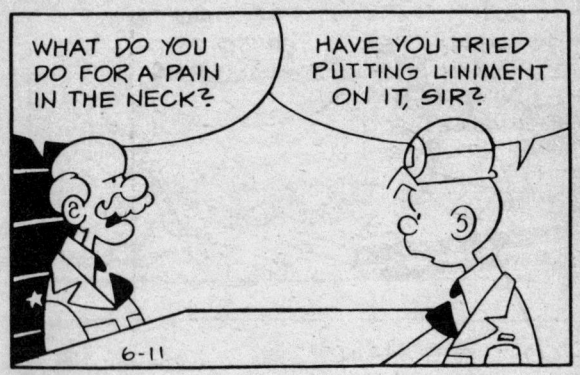

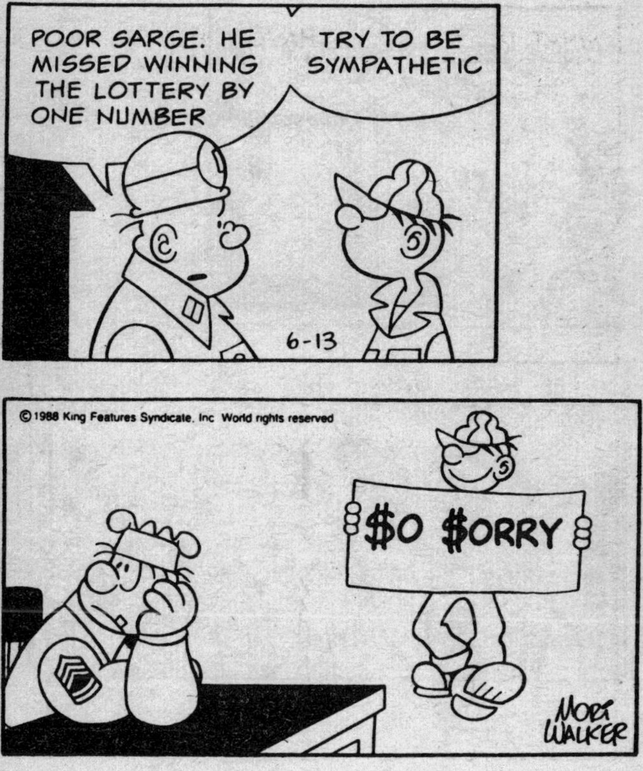
POOR SARGE. HE MISSED WINNING THE LOTTERY BY ONE NUMBER
TRY TO BE SYMPATHETIC
6-13
© 1988 King Features Syndicate, Inc World rights reserved
$O $ORRY
MORT WALKER

OH-OH! SGT. LOUISE LUGG IS INSPECTING AT FORMATION TODAY
SHE'S SUCH A STICKLER FOR DETAIL
6-14
© 1988 King Features Syndicate, Inc. World rights reserved
SNIFF SNIFF... WHAT KIND OF SHAMPOO IS THAT?
MORT WALKER